McNeil's
MOUNT HOOD

Wy'East THE Mountain
Revisited

By Fred H. McNeil
Revised edition 1990

Published by

The Zig Zag Papers
Zig Zag, OR 97049

Published by The Zig Zag Papers,
Box 247
Zig Zag OR 97049

Printed and bound in the United States of America

Book Design by Robert Reynolds
Cover Photo by Jim Running
Typesetting by Media Weavers

Library of Congress Catalog Card Number 89-51945

Publishers Cataloging-in-Publication Data

McNeil, Fred H.
   McNeil's Mount Hood

   Includes Index, Visitors Guide

   1. History
2. Mount Hood
3. Mountaineering
4. Winter Sports
I. Title

ISBN 0-9614498-7-X Softcover

To Mr. Malcolm Stuart
who alone remained
calm amid this
writing furor

Contents

Publisher's Note

In the raw, bluff world of the newsman Fred H. McNeil knew and understood the full meaning of a mountain's influence on men and women. He wrote with the feeling of one who lived it. These qualities we aim to preserve in this new edition of his 1937 book, *Wy'east, 'THE Mountain,'* now long out of print.

This first substantive history of Mount Hood gives a colorful account of the peak "that towers like a Guardian" (McNeil said) of the Oregon Cascades and the intricate human and geological chronicle of a volcano.

Wy,east was published by Philip L. Jackson, publisher of the *Oregon Journal* daily newspaper (now defunct). It was one of a long series on Northwest subjects which Jackson produced each year at Christmas. *McNeil's Mount Hood*, the new edition, honors Jackson too; for invaluable assistance in this production we thank Jim Running, Dave Falconer, Ed O'Meara, Al Monner and Herb Alden. We all worked with McNeil at *The Journal*, as did Tom McAllister, who is still writing outdoors for *The Oregonian* after 37 years. We also had generous help from John Eliot Allen, Ken Cameron, Carol Campbell, Carroll Davis, George Henderson, Glenn Ireland, Karen Mapes, Malcolm McNeil, Judith Platt, Pat Pringle, Bob Reynolds, Jean Stein, Linny and Dennis Stovall.

"Wy,east" was the timeless Indian name, and Jackson tagged the title "THE Mountain." McNeil had been a news reporter and editor for 25 years. As well, he was a mountaineer writing about men and women in experiences he knew first-hand. He spent much of his free time on Mount Hood; he worked one year for the U. S. Forest Service — in the Mount Hood National Forest, of course.

The 1980 eruption of Mount St. Helens reminds us that McNeil's mountain has seen the endless process of change in the years since 1937. Our "Afterword" chapter sketches some main events and trends of the intervening 53 years — events and changes which surely would have fascinated Fred McNeil.

We have tried to preserve and enhance the thought and words of a man born in the Nineteenth Century. We have rewritten some of his work in terms suited to this Century, now on the wane. In doing so we have reduced or eliminated certain passages whose relevance faded with time.

We sought to make more credible the heroic deeds of people of another age who met hostile conditions of life in a strange land of overwhelming beauty. Mostly they just did what they could to survive. They prevailed, and we strain to believe. In irony, if they could return, those sturdy Americans would question the pace and style of the lives we lead today.

I have changed certain errors and shadings in trying to enhance what McNeil wrote long ago; in doing so, other errors doubtless have crept in. For those I assume the blame. The credit for McNeil's fine writing is his. It was my pleasure to undertake this task, and my privilege to recommend this work from one who wrote a fraction of what he knew by experience and observation over a quarter-century.

Joe Stein
February 25 1990

Preface

The guardian Cascade peaks captivated Fred H. McNeil (1893–1958) from the day he arrived in Portland in 1912.

This 19-year old journalist, fresh from the Illinois prairie (he was born in Decatur) pursued and reported events on the peaks with a passion. He became personally involved in their protection as well as their development, especially for skiing.

He realized that these majestic peaks were more than scenic backdrops and challenging retreats. He also wrote of their economic worth in terms of tourism and recreation.

When not in the mountains his base was the *Oregon Journal* where he had a newspaper career of almost 45 years. He died the same year he retired from the paper.

From under his green editor's eye-shade McNeil kept an eye on both the copy rim and Mount Hood. His favorite peak, in regal isolation, dominated the skyline eastward across the Willamette River from the Journal Building newsroom windows on Front Avenue.

Reporters joked that an eruption on Mount Hood would only be exceeded by McNeil's reaction.

He had a crusted surface that sometimes intimidated newcomers, especially reporters who misspelled or who failed in Oregon geography, but he had a pillow soft interior.

He had so much to put into his own stories that he proved a lengthy writer, and when others edited him he would groan, "My God, you're killing it."

McNeil was a prolific reviewer of mountaineering literature and would bear down on the book with a black graphite pencil as he marked errors and transpositions. Some said he added half a pound of lead to a book not edited to his standards.

Edward F. O'Meara, later managing editor of *The Journal*, first worked under McNeil on the night copy desk, and O'Meara learned from the outset that downed airplanes or lost persons, mountain rescues and forest fires took precedence over all other news on McNeil's shift, particularly if they happened on Mount Hood.

Reporter Rolla Crick said that if he could combine the weather and Mount Hood in the same story, it was a cinch for a banner headline when McNeil was on the rim.

McNeil, a vigorous hiker, understood every topographic detail of the mountain, and he knew on a first name basis those members of the Wy'east Climbers, Mount Hood Ski Patrol, Crag Rats, Mazamas, Alpinees, Trails Club and Cascade Ski Club who came together for searches and rescues.

As the story broke McNeil pored over his collection of maps, interrogated the reporter on the phone and injected details and background from his wealth of mountain knowledge.

This newspaperman knew that in his adopted Oregon country there was romance, some tragic and some pleasant, in stories developed out of contact with the mountain wilds. He put outdoor adventures into the news.

His zealous interest in searches for those lost in the wilds may have stemmed from his own 1917 experience when he took a wrong turn on a Mazama annual outing to Mount Jefferson.

The base camp was at Pamelia Lake, but McNeil spent a frigid night in Jefferson Park where he fell asleep curled up so close to his campfire that he burned his pants. When searchers found the big man, he was too famished to walk until they brought food.

McNeil's fount of mountain lore developed early on when he joined the Mazamas in 1914 and used "c/o *The Oregon Journal*" for his mailing address.

He was with the Mazamas that August when their annual outing was held close by the Carbon and White River glaciers on the northeast side of Mount Rainier, and on the 1915 outing McNeil reported "Some Facts About Mount Shasta" for the Mazama annual.

Instead of social banter about the outing he was into the historic and geologic background, and he noted that Shasta's summit record box was "crammed full of books and papers of unusual character."

These included cards advertising stage lines running out of Sisson and McCloud, California, and dating back to 1874. McNeil said that the most interesting was a large volume of the Bible placed on the summit in 1882 by a minister who dedicated the fly leaf inscription "to the use of those who climb this mountain."

Signatures were scrawled from Genesis to Revelation with Scripture passages underlined where climbers found appropriate expressions for their feelings.

"A veritable circle of names surrounds the passage describing the journey of Moses to the top of Sinai to receive the commandments," wrote McNeil.

His personal commandment seems to have been to watch over and report on these fire cones of the Pacific Crest and to stimulate people's interest and enjoyment of them.

He was a working member of numerous annual outings, and recording secretary for the Mazamas to which his wife, Abby; son, Malcolm, and daughter, Judith, all belonged. [*He dedicated this book to his son, Malcolm Stuart McNeil.*]

He joined with other early climbers who foot-slogged upward before there was a road to timberline on Mount Hood. The climb began after the challenging drive over planks and through ruts to reach Government Camp.

They camped in the tent "hotel" at what was called Camp Blossom, enjoyed the campfire repast and songs, climbed to the summit the next morning, then dashed back down to Government Camp for the arduous return drive, to get home at midnight or later.

He had an ardent interest in skiing when it started to surge in the late 1920's. He was an early member and president of Cascade Ski Club which held its first jumping tournament at Multorpor Hill in 1929.

The club became the prime sponsor of downhill and slalom racing events on Mount Hood and supported a racing school and ski team for juniors.

McNeil's was a guiding hand when he chaired a 1930 organizational meeting of the six Oregon-Washington ski clubs to form the Pacific Northwest Ski Association (PNSA).

He was president those first five years and watched PNSA oversee ski competition as it developed from a handful of jumping tournaments through the beginnings of ski racing in the Pacific Northwest. Racing under international rules arrived at timberline on Mount Hood with the Far West Kandahar featuring downhill and slalom in the spring of 1940.

The PNSA became a powerful division of the National Ski Association, and McNeil was a vice president of the National where he chaired the public lands committee and expanded on his desire to see more developments for skiers.

In 1957 McNeil was named to the U. S. National Ski Hall of Fame in Ishpeming Michigan, because his actions and writings were an instrument that opened the mountains for Pacific Northwest skiers. He shares the Ski Hall of Fame with four other Mount Hood skiers:

- *Gretchen Fraser,* who stirred local pride with her 1948 Olympic gold medal, America's first in the special slalom event;
- *Don Fraser,* Gretchen's husband, who won the first Silver Skis Race at Mount Rainier in 1934 and was a member of the 1936 U. S. Olympic Ski Tam, and a National Ski Patrol organizer;
- *Barney McNab,* who organized the Mount Hood Ski Patrol; and
- *Hjalmar Hvam,* inventor of the first ski safety binding and a legendary combined jumper and racer.

McNeil always expected someone else would chronicle the story of Mount Hood, and then he is said to have done it in 14 furious days of writing while sequestered in a cabin on the Oregon Coast. He was a towering figure who leaped in and did things with zest. In winter he wore wool shirts, ski cap and loden coat to work.

I first encountered Fred McNeil when he recruited and trained forest lookouts and guards for the U. S. Forest Service in World War II. He took leave from *The Journal* to direct emergency manpower training for the forest fire lookouts which also served as a weather reporting and aircraft spotter system, at a time when the Japanese were thought to be just over the horizon.

Because of McNeil I spent my 17th summer as a fire lookout on a bald-top peak, Hager Mountain. This was also the lightning rod of the Silver Lake Ranger District, Fremont National Forest.

Ten years later I approached this editor whose very being could fly, at a glance out the window from his *Journal* desk, to Wy'east "The Mountain."

I was the green new outdoors writer.

I wanted his approval for a story about the ongoing closure of Lolo Pass road and all the country it tapped, almost a complete township, on the west and northwest flanks of Mount Hood.

Under the old Bull Run Division boundary it had been closed to public entry since 1892 by Presidential proclamation.

Portland's pure water came from the Bull Run River and not the glacial sources of Sandy River on Mount Hood. McNeil grasped the story's import instantly and made it more than an outdoor column.

McNeil had me ski through the locked gate and over Lolo Pass with Photographer Les Ordeman and Zig Zag District Ranger Jim Langdon.

That story of the mountain behind a locked gate started front page and had an inside photo page, subsequent followup stories and a supporting editorial.

Within weeks the Oregon Congressional delegation was aboard and the Chief U. S. Forester was involved. The gates to Lolo Pass opened.

McNeil was a mountain mover and shaker and, by lovely coincidence, the area opened in the old Bull Run division is where he is remembered in name with McNeil Point and McNeil Forest Campground on the headwaters of the Sandy River.

McNeil Point, at approximately 6000 feet elevation, or timberline on Bald Mountain Ridge, divides McGee Creek from the Muddy Fork Sandy River.

McNeil Point is about a quarter-mile above the Timberline Trail that circles Mount Hood, and it's marked by one of the old rock shelters built by the CCC (Civilian Conservation Corps).

This is the final resting place for Fred H. McNeil. His friends from the mountaineering and ski clubs and the Forest Service placed his ashes where he succumbed to what he called, "the mystic spell of the snowcap."

A favorite line of his from Browning said it:

"See the evening glow,
How sharp the silver spear heads charge
When Alp meets Heaven in snow."

Tom McAllister
February 25, 1990

Fred H. McNeil

Foreword

From the summit of Mount Hood, the view covers more history than from any other western peak. Almost at its northern base flows the Columbia river, which was a highway for centuries, first of the Indian and later, the white man. Within view to the northeast are the Celilo and the Long Narrows of the stream where lived and commingled during the fishing season the greatest Indian population on this continent.

Nearby, U. S. troops were stationed at Fort Dalles to guard the immigrant trains and the new settlements of the whites. Beyond can be seen the fields of fierce battling as the Indians sought to repel the invaders. To the west, at Vancouver, was the great establishment of the Hudson's Bay company, which dominated all the region early in the Nineteenth Century, with Dr. John McLoughlin, White Eagle, as the chief. Portland; Oregon City, the first territorial capital; Champoeg, where settlers formed the first local government of the Willamette valley under the Stars and Stripes; Salem, the Chemeketa council place of the valley tribes and later the state capital — all are within the sweep of the eye from the mountain top.

Far to the east are the Blue mountains, whence immigrants first saw Mount Hood as they neared their journey's end in the great trek across the plains to the Willamette. Their route may be followed along the Columbia to The Dalles, turning south, then westward along the pass of Barlow at the mountain base. Through the Sandy river valley beyond they pressed on to their goal. The primary baseline, one of the two first land measurements made in the Pacific Northwest, crosses the more distant spurs of Mount Hood on the north side. From this all other surveys of the region have been extended.

Not the highest of the Cascade peaks, Mount Hood is the most imposing. Its pyramid of rock and ice, sweeping to a sheer apex of noble proportions, is the predominant feature of the country. By many travelers Hood has been classed with the most beautiful mountains on the globe. The Cascade chain is studded liberally with peaks but where they attain their greatest heights the volcanos begin. They appear as objects alien to the wooded ridges. Without them the Cascades still would be listed among the major mountain ranges of the globe; with these huge spires and domes upon their crests they are unique.

So, from such Cascadian folds Mount Hood rises until its tip soars a mile above them. No other peaks cluster about to mask its sweeping curves. The monarch stands in regal isolation, fending away easy familiarity — to the beholder an object of veneration, almost of worship. To this distinctive presence a personality has been attributed that seems to extend a kind of character to each community within view and a feeling of exaltation to influence the life of every individual in its province.

More people climb this peak than any other on the continent. Many thousands have gone to the top and, these days, high accommodation makes it easy. This ceaseless trudging has defiled its majesty in no degree. There remains as always the bounds that dare not be trespassed. Despite this fair approach, dire retribution awaits those who venture too boldly too far.

The old newspaperman who ground out this volume has spent much of the past 25 years in avocational wandering through the hills and vales of the Pacific Northwest. In so doing he became a member of that horde who have succumbed to the mystic spell of the snowcap. With a great many others who are thus entranced, he has given hours to just looking at the mountain, fascinated ever by its stately profile, its lines, its colors and its moods. With much surprise he found that the greater task in compiling these chapters was deciding what to choose from the abundance of material that exists. Another book of equal length could be written without doubling on the episodes covered here, yet the whole story of Mount Hood — rather, of the interesting association of humanity with the mountain — would be incomplete. The existence of this prodigious record is itself evidence of the extraordinary interest and devotion Mount Hood holds for all who come near it.

Preparation of a book of the general character of subject matter undertaken here — scientific work, history and adventure associated with the mountain — would have been impossible without the assistance of many people. Such has been given generously, and to these collaborators the writer is sincerely grateful. There was Dr. Edwin Hodge, the geologist; Lije Coalman, beloved philosopher of the hills, who revealed the story of his life on Mount Hood; Tom Sherrard, a venerable of the Forest Service; Will Langille and his gracious family; Kenneth Phillips, scientist- engineer of the U. S. Geological Survey, who knew the glaciers and fumaroles; Clarence Orvell Bunnell, for the Indian legends; Nelly Pipes, librarian of the Oregon Historical Society; Joe Thomison, former editor of the Hood River *Glacier*, and Kent Shoemaker, Andy Anderson and others of the Valley.

Then there are those younger bloods of the peak, the Paytons and the Onthanks and the Darrs and all their ilk of the Mazamas and the Wy'easters, and figures of some of the mountain's most engaging tales. The library of the Mazamas with its excellent Mount Hood collection and the files of *The Oregonian* and *The Oregon Journal* were inexhaustible sources of material. Some mountain man or other, old and young, poked his head over the writer's shoulder as each chapter was produced. Each one contributed his share and has the appreciation of the compiler.

A writer is on delicate ground in recording events so recent that participants still survive. No two such persons ever see an occurrence alike. So here the chronicler's head is on the block over which the axes of the critics wave....

F.H.M.
Portland, Oregon
October 15, 1937

1.   The Klickitat Fire Legend

In The Beginning

Warrior heroes, fair ladies and their gods were greatly favored in the mythology of the American Indians. Ranking with the finest stories are the fire legends of the mid-Columbia River concerning three volcanic peaks. To the Indians they were Loo-wit, the gentle but cold maiden, Pa-toe (or Klickitat), the rough, good-natured giant, and Yi-east, the warrior whose passionate love caused a region to be transformed.

To us they are the graceful veiled cone of St. Helens that stands far west of the summit of the range, the lusty Mount Adams, whose head is forever buried in grief, and the proud, defiant Mount Hood, whose brow is high as he glares at his fallen brother across the Great River of the West. Between them, in the river's bed, lies the toppled Tomaniwus Bridge, span of amity, which Loo-wit had guarded.

There are several versions of the fire legend. One of the better known of these has Loo-wit as the maiden over whom the brothers fought, and in the last battle Klickitat broke his leg and was forced to retire. To the tribes east of the Cascades, however, there was still another young squaw for whose hand the sons of Soclai Tyee, the Great Spirit, hurled their fire.

Clarence Orvel Bunnell, who was born in the heart of this Indian country, heard from the natives their legends as far back as he can remember. The Indians, traveling to the fishing grounds at the Celilo, passed near his home on the bank of the Columbia; from their elders he gathered the stories in his 1933 book, *Legends of the Klickitats*, from which this account comes.

People lived on the shores of that sea which extended from the Cascades east to the Coeur D'Alene. The waters teemed with fish, game roamed the forests, and fruits and berries were abundant. On the meadows grew the camas food, and the trees furnished fuel. Everyone lived in peace and plenty. The trees, the animals and the birds were able to talk like people, and took part in the contests at the potlatches. Koyoda Spielei, the demigod, had given the people their mouths and was their supreme high priest, maker of laws and teacher of wisdom. To him even Pa-toe and Yi-east, sons of the Great Spirit, went with their problems.

Pa-toe and Yi-east dwelt on the westerly shore of the sea. Into a little valley between them, a Beautiful Squaw Mountain moved. She grew to love Yi-east, the lesser of the pair but she made him jealous by flirting with Pa-Toe, and both mountains fell madly in love with her. They began quarreling, although before they had been close friends as all good brothers should be. From growling and rumbling and stamping their feet to shake the earth, they became so angry that they spat ashes and fire, belching forth great clouds of black smoke so all the heavens were darkened. To the pleading of Koyoda they paid no heed. Discarding their fine white coats, they painted themselves and the surrounding country with streams of liquid fire, and hurled white hot rocks at each other.

When they finally tired of this foolish battle, their fiery coats were drab. The forests were burned away, the berries, fruit and camas destroyed, the game killed or in far flight. The people who survived had hidden in caves. The great Inland Sea was gone, taking with it the fish and water animals. During the fight a hole had been torn by the shaking of the earth in the range between the two mountains and through this the waters raced, wearing away more and more until there was a tunnel through which the river flowed under a great natural bridge.

Meanwhile Beautiful Squaw Mountain, in terror, hid in a cave where neither rival could find her. Each blamed the other for this and the fight was about to resume when Koyoda told the

Great Spirit what was going on. So he came to earth and stopped the battle, rebuking his sons for their wicked ways. He decreed that Beautiful Squaw Mountain should remain hidden always, where they could never find her. And he ruled that the bridge should stand as a covenant of peace between them, over which the people should pass to lay their prayers at the feet of the gods. If they fought he would cause the bridge to fall and each forever would have to stay on his own side of the river. A toothless old woman, in the form of a mountain, was left to guard the bridge so the brothers, seeing her, would always remember their folly and know that beauty in women is never permanent.

Follows here the story of how Koyoda and six braves explored the tunnel and the stream beyond in a great canoe, carried finally to the ocean as they searched to replenish the food supply of their starving people. They were aided by friendly coast Indians who persuaded the gulls and the seals to round up great schools of salmon, driving them back up the rivers. The gulls cried "klick-tat!" continuously as they kept the swarm moving. Once past the tunnel the gulls liked the country so well that they asked to remain and Koyoda changed them into Indians and caused them to settle about the base of Pa-toe. His name then was changed to Klickitat in their honor. This is why the Klickitat always claimed to be brothers to the gulls. The salmon, having learned the way, returned regularly in the the river, and the people thereafter always had plenty to eat.

After many years Beautiful Squaw Mountain became tired of her cave. The bats, then a tribe of proud, beautiful birds placed there as guards by the Great Spirit, came to love her and sympathize with her misfortune. They carried secret correspondence between her and Yi-east. But they were indiscreet and Yi-east was caught trying to get back across the bridge. The Great Spirit became angry with the faithless bats and ordered that they should be neither bird nor beast but the ugly semblance of each; and that they should fly only by night and hang by their heels in caverns by day — so they remain. However, he realized how lonesome Beautiful Squaw Mountain had been, and allowed her to remain out on her promise to be good.

Soon afterward, she and Yi-east asked the Great Spirit's consent to their marriage. He was sympathetic but refused, fearing Klickitat's rage. He warned them to break up their affair under pain of sending the maiden back to her cave. He promised to find a mate for the grumbling Klickitat, but in the press of other duties neglected it and affairs again became tense. Beautiful Squaw Mountain dressed drably, was most discreet, but the two mountains continued their old quarrel and her aloofness made it worse. They were held in check by the Great Spirit's threats, but one day when he was away in another part of the world, hostilities broke out. Again they stamped and shook the earth, darkened the skies with smoke, hurled white hot stones, cast off their robes of white and painted themselves with blazing colors. Again the people fled as the forests flamed and the game perished. Finally these giants threw so many stones and shook the earth so hard that the bridge fell in a great mass into the river.

The battle raged on until Klickitat won. Yi-east admitted defeat and renounced all claim on Beautiful Squaw Mountain. She knew she belonged to the victor and, heartbroken, went to Klickitat. At his feet she sank into a deep slumber from which she never awakened. She is known today as Sleeping Beauty, and you may see her lying just west of Klickitat Mount Adams, still dressed in her dark, drab clothes. Until then Klickitat had a high, straight head like Yi-east, but he loved Beautiful Squaw Mountain and her fate caused him so much grief that he dropped his head and has never raised it since.

During the battle Loo-wit, the bridge guardian, had done everything in her power to stop it. Failing in that she tried to save the bridge, and went down with the ruins when it collapsed. Badly burned and bruised by the flying hot rocks, she was heard moaning and crying by the Great Spirit when he hurried back, too late to prevent the disaster. Knowing how faithful she had been, he rescued Loo-wit, healed her wounds and told her that, as a reward, whatever she most desired would be granted. She asked to be made once more young and beautiful.

The Great Spirit replied that he could change her body and physical appearance, but not her mind. This was exactly as she wished, and the transformation occurred. She took her place among the great snow mountains, but being old in mind and spirit she was satisfied with her own cold beauty and did not desire companionship. So she withdrew from the main range and settled by herself far to the west where she remains today — aloof, unconcerned — the youngest and loveliest, yet the oldest of all the snow mountains.

Bunnell did not touch on a modern note of the later fortunes of the Sleeping Beauty. The U. S. Forest Service, seeking a link in its fire suppression system, hewed a trail across and up her features, dynamited off the tip of her nose and erected thereon a fire lookout station.

2. The Rise and Fall of a Peak

(This chapter summarizes the story of the building of Mount Hood as it was revealed to the expert eye of an eminent scientist by the formations of the peak and the region about it. It was prepared after an examination of the topical writings by, and interviews with, Dr. Edwin T. Hodge, professor of geology in the Oregon System of Higher Education.)

Mount Hood, the most massive and striking object of the Oregon Cascades, was erected long after the range was built. Within the past 7,000 centuries it was constructed by the internal fires of the earth, razed by global external forces, rebuilt, and again it is being reduced to ruins. The energy that twice has built the peak may restore the old proportions anew but the relentless attrition of sun's heat, wind, precipitation and frost in turn will attack it again.

Through such a prodigious span of years that they must be measured in millions, such mountains have risen and subsided like the billows of the sea. The forces within the earth have thrust them up. Erosion has been their worst enemy, cutting them down ruthlessly. Of the five great eras into which the history of the earth have been divided chronologically, we are living in the Cenozoic, yet it alone dates back to the time when most of the Pacific Northwest region was under the ocean. In the early Cenozoic times two great highlands stood, the Siskiyou in the southwest and the Shoshone in the northeast. Between them an arm of the ocean extended eastward to lap against the flanks of the Rocky Mountains. Erosion of the coast and the highlands, with a gradual lifting of the ocean floor, filled this vast basin. The sandstones thus created date from the latter part of the Eocene period, the time of the dawn of recent life.

Vulcanism (volcanic action) began in the succeeding period, the Eocene. There was then no sign of the Cascades, though a great number of vents west of the present axis of the range were hurling out quantities of pyroclastic materials, tuff and ash, to lay down those basic layers that we call the Eagle Creek formations because they have been found along the Columbia Gorge; here the cutting of the river has exposed the various deposits.

This volcanic activity continued into the Miocene period, but the character of the material ejected changed to liquid lavas, the outpourings of basalt that flowed in sheets (called by geologists "the flood") which spread out to build the plateau of central and eastern Oregon, Washington and Idaho. It buried to a depth of thousands of feet the products of explosive eruption that had preceded this quiet flow from fissures, rather than elevated cones. Still the Cascade range has not risen.

In the opening of Pliocene times that followed, there occurred a fracture of the earth's crust under the Pacific Ocean, close to and parallel to the crust. That was when the oceanic crust shoved under the continent. Most of the state of Oregon was gradually elevated east of the line of this offshore fault. Faulting also appeared in a line from north to south; it is traced along the Hood River valley and the line of the summit of the Cascades. The land west of it began to fold. The gigantic wrinkling of this movement is shown in the geological picture book of the Columbia Gorge. These folds formed the surface on which the Cascades were erected. Along this fault volcanic vents began pouring forth again — dust, bombs, cinders, ashes, much the same as those layers buried before by the basalt. Following these explosive ejections came more flows of liquid lava, the andesites. They continued until they had built the great elongated heap which we call the Cascades.

The first Mount Hood was built by the discharge of rocks and liquid lava from one of the vents along the High Cascade fault. It was a cone much higher than the one we see today, rising probably above 13,000 feet.

In this period, when the Cascades thrust their heads to altitudes higher than we now see, they immediately encountered the forces of erosion. As now, the prevailing winds then were from the northwest in the summer, southwest in the winter. They were humid winds, laden with moisture from passage over the Pacific; rain in the summer, frost and snow in the winter. In addition to expansion and contraction of each day, the sun's heat, the night's chill, were the forces at work. Erosion was greatest on the western slopes, and this is explained easily by the knowledge that the prevailing winds, from the west, brought the storms to add their bit in the tearing down process. This explains, too, the less abrupt canyons and gentler slopes on the east side of the Cascades as they merge into the high interior plateau.

Erosion destroyed part of this first Mount Hood, and the rest subsided in a down-dropped block (graben) between north-south faults. The Pleistocene or Glacial period had come, the Age of Ice. The Cascades had interposed a barrier to the humid winds that trapped their moisture. This was precipitated as rain or snow, in amounts vastly greater than today. Glaciers ate into this mountain and reduced it in places to the level of the surrounding plateau. The great water drainage system we now see (the Hood and Sandy Rivers) was formed by the reservoir where the mountain had been. This might have been a huge icefield.

From the midst of it, probably from the same volcanic vent that built the first mountain, the second peak rose (within 700,000 years past) in successive outpourings of lava. The rain of clinkers, cinders and bombs and the flooding of liquid lavas upon the glaciers and snowfields must have been a stunning spectacle. The mountain grew to a sharp-peaked cone and its height probably was around 12,000 feet, in horizontal dimensions much the same as the longer ridges today indicate, spurs like the cleaver down the east side of White River and a prolongation of the Barrett Crest. When this mountain stood as a nearly intact cone it must have been the time of the rain forests, which grew up its slopes to 9,000 feet. Over the lowlands the general heat was greater than today and massive stands of walnut, oak, willow and sequoia thrived. It was a day coeval with prehistoric man. There was an interlude then in the Age of Ice.

An interesting place to visit on the mountain today is the Stadter Buried Forest, on the south side of the spur which separates Reid from Zig Zag Glacier, at an elevation of 6,200 feet. The precise location is the north side of the north fork of the south fork of the Sandy River. The fossil forest lies beneath and on a mass of glacial material which in turn covers an andesite flow. Ends of the buried trunks protruding from the side of the spur led to the discovery in 1926 by Judge Fred W. Stadter. These trees are believed to be remains of the rain forest which existed when the mountain was slightly active, ejecting steam and causing many warm fog clouds and rain. They dissolved the glaciers or contracted them to small fields.

In 1988, Kenneth Cameron and Pat Pringle, U. S. Geological Survey, studied the Stadter Forest on a field trip. By precise measurements they placed it at the 5,850-ft. level, below the timberline. It is reached only by a 7-mile hike on the Timberline Trail to Paradise Park, thence northward angling uphill to the edge of the deep canyon draining the Zig Zag Glacier.

The geologists reported that the forest "is exposed across the canyon above the local treeline as a line of logs sticking out of the canyon wall, about 5 feet below the top of the wall on the upstream end and about 40 feet below the top [downstream].... [Some 30] logs of 1 to 2-ft. diameter are exposed....All are prone, aligned more or less due west, and show considerable abrasion....in extremely good state of preservation." They carbon-dated the logs back some 1,700 years, and wrote that the trees were buried not by glacial but eruptive action.

When vulcanism ended, the warm fogs and rains ceased and the usual cold precipitation, chiefly snowfall, produced ice fields too large to melt during the summers, and the glaciers developed again. The gravity movement of Zig Zag Glacier advanced upon the trees and wrenched them loose, to be carried several thousand feet down the mountain. Although the glacier drove far into the lowlands (traced to the lower valley of the Salmon River where a terminal moraine now stands) it did not carry the trees far, but deposited them in the ground moraine (under the glacier). The ice stream then retreated, leaving behind a great amount of debris, and much of this still covers the forest remains.

After the recession of the glacier far up the slope again, waters from its melting began cutting their V-shaped canyons; eventually the walls of this one were hewn back enough to expose these trunks. Indications are that a much greater mass of this forest remains under the glacial till.

In these times occurred, it is believed, Mount Hood's latest explosion which tore off the whole south side of the cone. Fragments of this blast are to be seen on all the slopes, but chiefly on the south side. Remaining afterward was something of the shape we see today. The cone's sharp tip vanished and left the cuplike depression in the top that climbers now see.

The huge gaps in the southern wall of this so-called crater were not blown out, as many have concluded, but removed by erosion, chiefly by work of the two chief south side glacier heads, Zig Zag and White River. The crater bowl filled with snow and this, tumbling over, aided in tearing down the wall through which the glaciers reached to tap the *neve* within the bowl and attacked the north and east walls of the crater. Crater Rock is one of the old solidified "plugs" in the volcano's core, or drain pipe, through which its discharges were forced.

Mount Hood is not "dead," in the meaning of the term extinct volcano. It is, instead, still active, as the steaming fumaroles indicate. It is more active, indeed, than was Mount Vesuvius in the days before its lavas poured over Pompeii, when peasants were tilling lands far up its slopes. The evidence, as shown by the fumaroles, is held to be positive that there is "life" yet in Oregon's highest and most stately mountain.

So remains the possibility of further vulcanic eruption.

Events proved McNeil's prophetic words. The 1980 eruption of Mount St. Helens gave geologists a wealth of knowledge about the composite volcanos of the Cascades, including Mount Hood.

3.   As a City Sees It

When the meteorologists' so-called "summer high" arrives over the Pacific in mid-spring, the westerly trade winds give the Northwest the finest season of the year. Spring, if it has been laggard, appears then. Over the lustrous color of new growth, fat cumulus clouds cruise grandly through the sky. Winter rains have cleansed the atmosphere of forest fire smoke and the dust that arid winds lifted from the fields the autumn before. The atmosphere is tempered only by blue haze upon the distant hill; it seems to accentuate and magnify those objects that it drapes.

This, let us say, is the setting one early June morning on the slopes where Portland is built. We await the sunrise. Great folds of mountains provide a rippling horizon from north to south as far as the eye will carry. Superimposed on this line are five mighty peaks, the three called Guardians of the Columbia and two others that seem to flank them. At far left is Mount Rainier, the ponderous dome that overlooks Puget Sound. Apparently near it and next in line is the truncated cone of St. Helens, youngest of the volcanoes of the Northwest. In distant view the symmetry of its smooth lines seem unbroken; one must approach close to perceive the cirques, aretes and cliffs that erosion has carved. Because it stands well west of the main divide of the Cascades, almost all of this mountain's graceful beauty is in view.

McNeil here writes of St. Helens's appearance before the Great Eruption of 1980.

Peering over loftier folds of the Cascades, and much farther away, is Mount Adams. From Portland we can see the upper one-third of this mountain, which has a ponderous two-mile summit.

If we are high enough above the housetops where the look mountain-ward is unimpaired, we see the Cascades to their bases, with the piedmont inclined toward us. A sharp break in the range discloses the Gorge of the Columbia. Lifting our gaze southward from this cleft, we observe that the line rises gradually but surely as the dark forested profile changes to snow. Then an upward soaring curve carries the eye to the tip of Mount Hood.

With no lesser peak intervening, all of its pyramid form is visible down to where the rib-like buttresses, hewn by the glaciers, meld into the forests of the lesser hills. Like St. Helens, Mount Hood once must have presented the aspect of the perfect cone, but volcanic explosion blew out a great segment of its crest. The debris of this titan blast remains strewn over its slopes today, and the present summit is a point some distance down the north side of what was the top in a preceding age. So, looking from the city, the observer sees a lopsided figure, as if a giant hand had shoved the top far to the north.

From Hood's southern base the eye's sweep covers more of the rugged Cascade skyline until it reaches the gaunt, cowl-like tower of Mount Jefferson, hovering above the lesser heights that bound the basin of the Clackamas River.

It is not strange that Portlanders give Mount Hood a reverence that borders on devotion. Like the Great White Throne of Utah's Zion National Park, the noble purity of its colors — white of snow and glaciers, ruddy rocks and green fingers of forest on its flanks, together with the majestic beauty of its sculpture — are forever fascinating. Even though residents of two states share in the glory of its presence, Mount Hood still is regarded as their own by prideful Portlanders. They see it there — not even in their own county — as a part of the city, as much so as those hills on which Portland is built.

In the City of Roses one does not easily get away from the mountain. In nearly every east-west extending street it is in view. One may pause in the turmoil of downtown business canyons to gaze at the distant pile of rock and ice and snow, and feel its thrill.

Homes are built with windows framing the peak. Eyes may turn from the piled business desk to rest upon the cool grandeur of this mass standing in the east. From the Willamette bridges, if skies are clear, it is ever there.

In early days travelers to the Willamette settlements saw the mountain long before they reached centers of habitation. Mount Hood always was a magnificent spectacle for the Hudson's Bay company colony established by Factor John McLoughlin where Vancouver Barracks, on the north bank of the Columbia, now stands. The "voyageurs," descending on the river from the Rocky Mountains, saw Mount Hood long before they approached the Gorge through which the Columbia breaches the Cascades. For travelers going up the river from the Pacific, the peak seemed, and seems today, to rise from the middle of the broad stream.

For those who gaze often and long at the mountain, and know its every line, there is the happy paradox of an unchanging object that never looks the same. Sometimes it appears high and harsh and cold, wearing a glowering austerity, warning away those who would come near. More often though, the mien is gentle, a warmth and softness beckoning all to come close. In winter when the east wind roars it stands in stark, marble-like bleakness, menacing, repelling. In the dawn of such days it is a grim silhouette against a bright sky.

But in the spring when the northwest wind blows, the white is a mantle of shining warmth, and its rocks seem to glow as if the mountain were calling its friends to return. The night fogs over lakes and marshy places rise as the sun warms them; they break into fat cumuli that hover about, bumping lazily into glaciers and rocky walls. For them the peak is a mooring mast.

The high snow freezes at night if the sky is clear, and the tiny rivulets are stilled. As the day advances the sun's rays unlock them again. Then resumes that summer melody of the crisp clicking of falling water droplets heard on every mountain blanketed by eternal ice.

In these first clear days of spring we see the mountain with an almost unbroken robe of white, the deep snows extending miles below its timberline into the forest. The colors only vary where the morainal wedges and the cliff faces, with flanks too steep to hold the snow, remain in gray and brown; in other areas, heat from below keeps them free of snow all winter. But soon, the gentler slopes above the upper fringe of forest growth emerge from the white. They green a bit, as the sturdy grasses and shrubs flourish for a brief season. Steadily the snows retreat upward until, in midsummer, they form a short cape over Mount Hood's shoulders. Glaciers then, bared again to their perpetual ice, are greenish gray aprons sprawled over its flanks.

When summer is long and dry even the cape disappears and rock is exposed to the very crest, ice remaining only in the deep glacial gullies that are shaded from the sun's full heat. Often now there will be a dull reddish cast over the mountain, preponderantly so on slopes of lava debris. The mountain's brilliance as a spectacle dims in such season. Forest fires are the inevitable consequence of dry weather, and the pall of smoke thickens day by day. Into this the mountain fades until it disappears. Sometimes one may stand at its very foot and not see the peak above. Even at dawn its bulk will not be a shadow against the murky sunrise.

In recent years urban smog and the smoke of field burning in the Willamette Valley have added more to the murk than forest fires have. — Editor

Occasional summer storms will bury it in clouds, later to emerge with the dark slopes attired in snow. This will vanish, perhaps in a day. Before the autumnal equinox, though, the snow resumes conquest. A sifting first appears over the loftiest rocks. Week by week this drapery thickens as it advances downward until it touches the forest. Each succeeding storm deepens it, filling out hollows, softening ridges, ironing away shadows as drifts fill the swales.

When the mountain is in showy mood there is no person so lacking in emotion as to escape its fascinattion. It comes when seen through the ghost-like crest reflecting the brilliance of the full moon. The heart leaps when its shadow springs out of the black night as summer lightning flashes along the horizon. Or when the peak is a flagpole from which long plumes of vapor stream away — certain portent of the tempest bound soon to enfold it and the surrounding country.

Again, on certain days of spring and autumn when watchers assemble on the heights to see the rising sun, in apparent motion, roll up the very line of northern slope. In all the world what other city is situated so precisely as to afford this stunning scene?

And finally the alpenglow. You must live in or near mountains to not merely see, but feel the alpenglow, the strange, lustrous rosy light bathing the high snowpeak at evening. It appears just when the sun drops below the horizon, an effulgence of color — not peach not pink not salmon, darker than these yet not somber and less dark than a ruby. One despairs of attempting to describe this ethereal glory over the high snows. Materiality departs; you are captured by a spiritual presence in this staging of one of Nature's most sublime offerings. As the sun sinks farther and farther, the band of rosy light ascends until, at last, it touches only the tip of the mountain. Suddenly you see the luminescence in the sky above and the snow and rocks below, bereft of radiance, now appearing bleak and cold. And brooding darkness enfolds the forests.

And if you have lived in those high forests, where the stubby, whitebark pines whip their withy boughs against the darkening sky you know the nighthawk is winging through the aisles of trees. He is alighting to wallow luxuriantly on the needle-littered ground, warmed by the sun that departed moments before.

4. The Beacon

Mount Hood and the Columbia River, even as they are situated side by side geographically, have figured side by side in the history of the Oregon Country. The river and the mountain were discovered together. It was from the bosom of the Great River of the West that the peak dominating the Oregon skyline was first seen by a member of the white race.

The finest songs, the most beautiful pictures and the most captivating stories of Oregon have been penned and painted around this combination of splendid snowpeak and mighty Columbia. The first great highway in the Northwest was built along the river toward the mountain. A later extension to encircle Mount Hood enables throngs of visitors from all the world to join with residents in enjoyment and appreciation of the snow giant of the Oregon Cascades.

Mount Hood stands for Oregonians as a monument to their pioneers and a tower of inspiration for their successors. The men and women who toiled across the Great Plains and the Rockies in the immigrations of the 19th century past, knew of the white pyramid pointing to the sky. They yearned for the day when, in tortuous descent of the Blue Mountains of eastern Oregon they might see its distant tip, perhaps in sunset's rosy glow. It meant the end of the battle with dangers on the Oregon Trail — hostile Indians, hunger, thirst, disease — and descent into green valleys of promise on the Pacific shore.

To them the mountain was a beacon of welcome, a pillar of friendliness. Passing it they put the menace of the wilderness behind at last. Ahead, friends awaited; opportunity, life, love — all these in the green western valleys past the Cascades.

Discovery of the river and the mountain came in the same year by separate parties. The river's mouth was found by Captain Robert Gray, a Yankee, who named it for his ship, the *Columbia Rediviva* Sailing the Pacific in the fur trade he crossed the river's bar on May 11 1792.

When British Navy Captain George Vancouver, then anchored in Puget Sound, learned that Captain Gray had found the Columbia, he sent off Lieutenant William E. Broughton in the armed tender Chatham. In the river Broughton anchored in what is now Astoria Bay October 24 1792. On that day, with his crew in two boats, he rowed upstream, passing the confluence of the Willamette, beyond where the Hudson's Bay company would later open the Fort Vancouver trading post. He went on to a point above what is now Washougal, Washington, close by the lower end of the great gorge of the river through the Cascades.

Broughton discovered Mount Hood on this voyage. Breasting the strong current he and his men first saw Mount St. Helens a few days out of their Astoria anchorage. For a time thereafter he was confused when another great snowpeak appeared, apparently rising in the river. Plainly, there were two peaks, St. Helens well to his left, the other ahead. On October 30 1792 he named the other Mount Hood, after Lord Samuel Hood of the Royal Navy.

Early Americans called the Cascades the Presidential Range and Mount Hood, Mount Washington. Neither of these names stuck. When Captains Meriwether Lewis and William Clark, exploring the newly-acquired Louisiana Purchase, saw the mountain from the east, they thought they had made a discovery. Soon after passing the mouth of the Snake River, Captain Clark, on October 19 1805 ascended a cliff about 200 feet above the Columbia. From there he saw to the west "a very high mountain covered with snow." He supposed it to be Mount St. Helens, "laid down by Vancouver as visible from the mouth of the Columbia." But from that point in eastern Washington, Captain Clark could not see St. Helens; the peak doubtless was Mount Adams, which, on the other hand, because of obscuring hills, well might have been overlooked by Broughton.

Continuing the account of that day, Captain Clark wrote that there was another mountain "of a conical form whose top was covered with snow," in a southwest direction. This was Mount Hood and it was the first of the many views the explorers had of it. When they reached that dangerous trough later known as the Long Narrows, they called it the Falls or Timms Mountain. But by the time they passed the "Quicksand" (now "Sandy") River, a stream that Lieutenant Broughton had reported 13 years before, they decided the peak was indeed Mount Hood.

Persistently but excusably, these explorers erred between Adams and St. Helens. When west of the Cascades and seeing St. Helens to their north, for the first time, they assumed they were merely looking from a different angle at Captain Clark's "very high mountain," which certainly was Adams.

After wintering near the mouth of the Columbia, Lewis and Clark returned upriver. On April 3 1806 Captain Clark discovered far to the southeast "a mountain which we had not yet seen." This he named Mount Jefferson.

The story of the exploration and settlement of Oregon, as available to us in original documents, abounds in references to Mount Hood. They indicate what a dominating feature the peak was to these early adventurers. The great wilderness — without road or trail except those of Indians and deer — was poorly mapped even to the most important geographic features. Eager travelers, fur trappers seeking wealth, prospectors, traders, scientists, missionaries, farmers, all passed by.

Some of these had no eye but for the object of their quest, others were illiterate and left no record. But many others set down their stories of privation and danger on the plains, of struggle in the mountains, adventures across the great Canadian routes and down the Columbia, of commercial exploits in the Sandwich (Hawaiian) islands and China; of pestilence at the Isthmus of Panama, and hurricanes around Cape Horn. They penned these tales in grand or modest style, rude or scholarly, and left them in every part of the world. And they wrote with great enthusiasm for the Cascades.

After Lewis and Clark came the expedition in 1811 of David Thompson, geographer of the Canadian North-West Company. He saw the Celilo falls when they were submerged by high water in the Columbia, and his journal refers to views of Mount Hood from various points along the river.

David Douglas, the young Scottish botanist for whom the

Douglas fir tree is named, came through the region in the 1820s. After Lewis and Clark he is regarded by many as the most important visitor of this period. Douglas was sent out by the Royal Horticultural Society; he entered the river April 19 1825.

At first Douglas held the opinion that Mount Hood could not be climbed, yet there is evidence that, eight years after writing this, he made an attempt to reach the summit. In his *Journal* (a volume too little known to our people) he wrote of his voyage up the river to the new Hudson's Bay Company post at Vancouver:

"On the south, toward the headwaters of the Multnomah [Willamette] which are supposed to be in a ridge of snowy mountains which run in a southwest direction from the Columbia, the view is fine. A very conspicuous conical mountain is seen in the distance far exceeding others in height; this I have no doubt is Mount Jefferson of Lewis and Clark; two others equally conspicuous are observed, one due east and one to the north, the former Mount Hood, the latter Mount St. Helens of Vancouver. Their height must be very great (at least 10,000 to 12,000 feet), two-thirds are continually enwrapped in perpetual snow. I have scarcely perceived any difference in the diminishing of the snow (now August). In June I was within a few miles of Mount Hood. Its appearance presented barriers that could not be surmounted by any person to reach the summit."

A London publication of 1835–36, *The Companion to The Botanical Magazine*, contains the only reference to Douglas's attempted climb. He nearly perished June 13 1833 in an accident on the Fraser River in British Columbia when his boat carried over a waterfall. He lost all his records, his diary and botanical journal, instruments and many botanical specimens.

Hence there remains no detailed account of Douglas's journey later that year, but the *Companion* account contained a letter to the editor by one Archibald McDonald, of Hudson's Bay Company, saying Douglas had told him of his movements that summer. With Pierre Pambrun, Walla Walla, he had made occasional "journeys to the Blue Mountains and finally attempted the ascent of Mount Hood." Nowhere is there any enlargement of this statement, unless in the carefully guarded company archives in London. It would be of great interest for us to know what he found in exploring the snowpeak in 1833.

Among Hudson's Bay reports is a vague story that two French voyageurs journeyed inland from the Columbia, probably along the Hood River, until they reached the ice fields of the "Montague de Neige," presumably stepping on Eliot Glacier or the supporting snow-covered slopes, perhaps about 1818.

Peter Skene Ogden, who at 32 was Hudson Bay's chief trader west of the Rockies, was enthralled by the great snowpeaks, and he traveled near them all. Starting from Walla Walla (Fort Nez Perce then) November 21 1825 with a large group of trappers and hunters, he swung through central and eastern Oregon and back to the Snake River. His journal reveals that on December 5 they were in the high country north of Tygh Valley. They had descended the Columbia, crossed the Deschutes, then struck southward up Fifteen-Mile Creek to where "we finally got out of th hills." On this day he saw "a grand and noble sight — Mount Hood bearing due west, Mount St. Helens and Mount Nesqually (Adams) northwest, covered with eternal snow and in a southerly direction other lofty mountains in form and shape of sugar loaves. At the foot of all these mountains were lofty pines which added greatly to the grandeur of the prospect."

On that day the party crossed Tygh Creek and White River. Both "appeared to take their rise from a mountain not far and covered with snow." They found the streams in freshet and the water so muddy they could scarcely swallow it. On an 1814 map, in Biddle's edition of the Lewis and Clark *Journal* White River appears as the "Skimhoox."

Captain Nathaniel J. Wyeth, a New Englander, had dreams of a trading empire beyond the Rockies. From a boat on the Columbia on his first expedition to the Oregon country he saw ahead, on October 20 1832, "a large snowy mountain, southwest by west, called by the French 'Montague de Neige,'" and on the 26th "we passed the high mountain covered with snow.... It is on the left of the river and is a more stupendous pile than any of the Rocky Mountains. It is called the Snow Mountain."

Hall J. Kelly, the visionary Boston schoolmaster who early brought before the American people the importance of Oregon occupation and settlement, in 1831 published a prospectus for colonists which included plans for a trading town on the peninsula at the confluence of the Multnomah (Willamette) and the

Columbia. Kelly wrote a "Geographical Sketch of That Part of North Americas Called Oregon." "Mount Hood," he said, "called by the Indians 'Timm,' rises in the form of a sugar loaf to a considerable height. Its top is destitute of trees and covered with snow." (The name "Timm" is probably a diminutive of the Celilo Indians' "Tum–Tum.")

Although amusing to us now, Kelly concluded that "St. Hellens" was the greatest of the "guardian peaks, rising to a stupendous height." In fact St. Helens is the smallest, but from the lower Columbia, among the short surrounding ridges it would appear much higher to the early visitor.

Lewis and Clark first called the Cascades the Presidential Range and Kelly used this title on his highly confused map. The mountain on the south side of the Columbia he called Mount Adams, yet his journal referred to the same peak as Mount Washington; and it shows his Mount Washington to be our St. Helens. In another version he has all the high volcanoes named for deceased presidents — Mount Baker as Tyler; Rainier as Harrison; St. Helens, Adams; Three Sisters, Madison, and Shasta, Jackson.

In the written record, Ogden was the first to identify Adams as a separate mountain, but he called it Nesqually. Kelly makes no mention of that.

Captain John C. Fremont first saw Mount Hood October 23 1843 while descending the west slope of the Blue Mountains. In the journal of his 1843–44 expedition through California and Oregon, when near the mouth of the John Day River he wrote, "Mount Hood is glowing in the sunlight this morning." On November 13, on return from Vancouver to The Dalles, the journal notes:

"Whenever we came in contact with the rocks of these mountains we found them volcanic, which is probably the character of the range; and at this time two of the great snowy cones were in action. On the 23d of the preceding November St. Helens had scattered its ashes, like a fall of snow, over The Dalles of the Columbia, 50 miles distant. A specimen of these ashes was given to me by Mr. Brewer, one of the clergymen at The Dalles."

Proceeding south a short time later from The Dalles along Fall (now Deschutes) River, Fremont alludes several times to Mount Hood. While encamped at "Taigh Prairie" (Tygh Valley) he wrote of it as "an old acquaintance."

5. Opening the Pass

Mount Hood wagon routes for access to the Willamette Valley came into use in 1845 as a protest of immigrants. The pioneers defied the high tolls they were charged for moving freight and stock from The Dalles by boat on the Columbia River. A cattle drover's trail lay along the Columbia's south bank to Hood River, thence up the valley of the west fork, over what is now known as Lolo Pass, to the head of the Sandy River valley.

In the deep hills between the Sandy and the Columbia is the valley of the Bull Run, a land reserve for Portland's water supply. For a score or more miles west of Mount Hood, the three streams, Columbia, Sandy and Bull Run, flow generally parallel. The Bull Run enters the Sandy, which, farther on, takes a sharp bend to the right to empty into the Columbia. The Bull Run is said to have been named from the fact that cattle escaping from drives over Lolo Pass went over the high divide into its valley and became wild in that watershed.

The immigrant company of Samuel K. Barlow, which started from Illinois, reached The Dalles late in 1845. Barlow, seeing Mount Hood first from the Blue Mountains, observed a notch indicating a possible pass just to its south. He chose to break a path of his own across the Cascades, saying, "God never made a mountain without some place to go over it." At The Dalles Barlow heard the pass was used as a stock trail as was Lolo Pass on the north. To the dismay of missionaries he chose the southern route. A mountain road at that point had not been thought of.

A train of 7 wagons and 19 persons filed out of The Dalles September 24 1845 and proceeded southward along the Deschutes, crossed the White River, then turned west toward the Cascades.

On October 1 came another immigrant, Joel Palmer, an Indiana farmer of marked capacity for leadership. He too saw the dearth of boats available, the hundreds of waiting immigrants, and the scarcity and high price of food. He resolved to follow Barlow, leading a train of 23 wagons. Along the White River the two men met and joined forces. They organized working parties and began construction of the road — hewing a path through thick brush and in some places, almost impenetrable forest. Having only axes and saws, they did much of the clearing by burning.

Palmer and Sam Barlow's son William rode ahead to scout a way for wagons across the divide. The season was growing late and they risked being snowed in; they agreed to cache wagons and gear on the east side of the pass, and the company would proceed with the stock. About five miles south of what we now know as Barlow Pass they built a shelter and left William Berry there as guard for the winter. The party encountered great hardships, but they were relieved when the younger Barlow went on ahead and returned with a pack train of provisions from Oregon City.

Laurel Hill, unlike the fine road we know today, was then a place of horrible memory for these immigrants. Of the many hardships they endured, it stands out as the worst. There is abundant record of the woe it caused. In 1937, as we drive it in comfort, we can recall a score of years ago when we said the same thing of the hill. As the only route to Mount Hood's south side, it was a rough approach. We still see the old tollgate — happily unused — the cabin of the Barlow and succeeding road companies, and substantial evidence of the old wagon trail.

Bad as it was, the Barlow road was an important factor in the settlement of western Oregon. "Its construction," wrote Judge Matthew P. Deady, "contributed more toward the prosperity of the Willamette Valley and the future state of Oregon than any other achievement prior to the building of the railways in 1870."

Palmer was the first white man to go high on Mount Hood. He forged ahead with William Barlow and a man named Lock to seek the pass — on a mission far more serious than climbing a mountain. They scouted the Indian trail, and found its route out of the question for wagons.

The Palmer route in the first hours is not known exactly because he wrote of the Deschutes branch and a branch of the branch, with few names attached to his landmarks. After scrambling through thick stands of cedar, they came to a long open section and, at its head, beheld Mount Hood from base to tip. They were looking up the broad, glaciated valley of White River. The Indian trail across the mountains lay along there.

Ascending in a northerly direction, the trail traversed a ravine on snow; they were at timberline. Then, Palmer wrote, they went on around the mountain, "crossing strips of snow" to a deep canyon (doubtless that of the Zig Zag River). Palmer wrote that it was "cut out by the mountain." A "precipitate cliff" prevented passage around its upper margin. This was the face we now call Mississippi Head. Palmer judged the ravine was 3,000 feet deep. They crossed it to find members of the party who had gone ahead driving the immigrants' cattle. It is easy to believe this camp was the beautiful spot we know today as Paradise Park.

On October 12 1845 they started up the mountain "heading the deep ravine." They meant to go high enough to see if a pass were visible. They followed "a grassy ridge to where it became barren." Here Lock and Barlow paused, saying they could not get around the head of the ravine, but Palmer later remarks they were wearing heavy boots, and pioneer boots, we know, were weighty and stiff. That is explanation enough for anyone who has done any hiking. But Palmer himself wore moccasins.

When his partners lagged, Palmer kept going, "climbing a cliff of snow and ice." Although he had soled his moccasins a few days before, they gave out and he was almost barefooted on the snow. He tried to exhort his companions to come along but they moved slowly, and Palmer could not wait because of his exposed toes. He went on up the snowfields for another mile. There he waited for the others, but in vain. He shouted and rolled stones down the mountain, then continued his climb.

If Palmer was reasonably accurate in his estimate of traveling a mile and more above timberline, he must (depending on direction) have gone close to the base of Illumination Rock or high on the Triangle Moraine. He mentioned nothing about the effects of altitude. Apparently he noted none of the novel sensations that high climbers sometimes encounter. He was intent on finding, not a route up the mountain, but a way around it for the band of weary travelers far down in the forest.

After rolling stones down the slope he wrote, "I then went round to the southeast side, continually ascending." Most of the time he was peering at the country to the south, and said he was "fully of the opinion we could get through." It is clear he gave thought to the ascent of Mount Hood because he wrote:

"The opinion heretofore entertained that this peak could not be ascended to the summit I found to be erroneous. I, however, did not arrive at the highest peak but went sufficiently near to prove its practicability. I judge the dimensions of this peak, at the point where the snow remains the year around, to be about three miles. At the head of many of the ravines are perpendicular cliffs of rocks apparently several thousand feet high; and in some places these cliffs rise so precipitately that a passage around them is impracticable. I think the southern side affords the easiest ascent. The dark strips observable from a distance are occasioned by blackish rock so precipitous as not to admit of the snow lying on it.

"There is no doubt but any of the snow peaks upon the range can be ascended to the summit."

From his high vantage point, Palmer observed in this accurate account of the physical features of the south side of Mount Hood, that the waters of the "deep ravine" of the day previous formed the head of the Sandy River. The Zig Zag is a branch of the Sandy, encountering it not far from the southwest base of the peak, and in his position on the southern slope he could not see across the intervening heights to the west side, where the Sandy's principal sources pour from the Reid and Sandy Glaciers. Down the stream he thought was the Sandy he could see about 15 miles, where the view was cut off by high ridges.

Another stream he saw in the low country directly south which he "judged to be the headwaters of the Clackimas." It disappeared to the south between two ridges connected by a "low gap with this peak." This low gap may well be accepted today as the site of Government Camp. Through there, travel over the Barlow Road was soon to flow westward. But the river he took to be the Clackamas could have been no other than the Salmon, which is yet another branch of the Sandy system.

Like the Bull Run, no part of the Clackamas River system rises on Mount Hood, although many believe both streams have sources on the mountain slopes. Quite likely the snow on which Palmer stood later was destined to be water of the Salmon River, and it is possible that he was actually on the ice sheet which in 1924 was revealed to be a glacier later named for him.

After his climb far up the southern face, Palmer began to feel the pangs of hunger. He had no food "save a small biscuit." Rations in the past few days had been meager. He also had 25 miles to cover in returning to the men working on the road. He began the descent then, crossing crevasses of the type that mountaineers call "blind," the openings being covered by a thin lid of snow left after the mass beneath has melted. These, he admits, presented alarming problems, but soon they were behind him and he saw his companions on the east side of the Zig Zag ravine. He rejoined them for the hike down through the forest to one of the meadows he had seen from the snowfields. A beautiful stream ran through it in "a southeast direction." They ate their biscuits and whortleberries found in the meadow, then went on to the White River valley. Finally, late at night they reached the road-builders' camp.

"Although not often tired, I was willing to acknowledge that I was near being so," Palmer wrote in concluding his narrative of that memorable day.

A few days later he led the party across the timberline trail. This time they encountered rain which higher up turned to snow, which covered the ground as they pushed on westward toward the Sandy valley. They rode saddle horses with their gear on pack animals. Their route off the mountain probably was past Paradise Park down Lost Creek to the Sandy. The route of Barlow's road, begun the next year, was far to the south of them.

There is little doubt that Joel Palmer's account of his exploit on the mountain influenced the first climbers, in the next decade, to follow the route he had helped to pioneer.

6. The First Ascents

The debate over who was first to climb Mount Hood's highest point has almost ended. A few diehards still hold that a party of which Samuel Dryer was the leader completed the ascent in 1854. A vastly greater number — and to this writer it is clear that the evidence is on their side — believe that initial climbing honors belong to the quartet who flung to the summit breeze an American flag on the afternoon of July 11 1857.

There appears no ground to doubt that Dryer and his followers did go very high on the peak, beyond any point previously reached, and were on a passage which, if followed out, would have taken them to the tip. But Dryer's chronicle does not indicate conclusively that this was done. He made the flat assertion that the party had completed the ascent but his account falls short in identifying and corroborating details.

For an interesting sidelight, Dryer was the owner and editor of the *Weekly Oregonian*, forerunner of Portland's great daily newspaper, while one of the four who climbed in 1857 was his employe, Henry Lewis Pittock. Young Pittock and his companions were given an editorial lashing by Dryer for coming back with the assertion that they had made the ascent, and for insinuating that he had not. (A few years later Pittock, who had become manager of the paper, took it over from Dryer as payment for debts.)

Of the climb by the quartet of which Pittock was a member, there can be no doubt. Their route is described carefully. A description of this expedition by the Rev. T. A. Wood is one of the most lucid and interesting accounts of mountaineering ever penned. The Dryer narrative is remiss in substantiating detail. If he did go to the uppermost point, then the credit denied him is an injustice which must be charged to his failure to tell the story completely.

Professor L. J. Powell organized the party of 1857. With him were W. L. Chittenden, J. J. Deardorff, William Buckley, Wilbur Cornell, Dr. and Mrs. J. S. Glenn, Miss Chittenden, the minister and Pittock. They rode horses to Summit Prairie, and the entire party started at 7:30 am — a late hour to begin climbing a major peak, especially from a point so distant as Summit Prairie from the top. They carried a spirit lamp and alcohol for making tea, a flag and flagstaff, but no sun glasses nor grease paint.

Soon after reaching the first snowfields, Miss Chittenden dropped out. At or near Crater Rock, a place where many climbers regularly quit, Mrs. Glenn decided she had had enough, and Dr. Glenn elected to remain with her. Soon the other climbers were near a cave from which came sulfur fumes; this must have been along the hogsback from Crater Rock to the summit wall, for here, the Wood diary notes, "the remaining part of the climb seemed almost perpendicular." At its base, he wrote, there was a "deep chasm, like a horseshoe, through which we passed." This probably was the Big Crevasse.

From this point, kicking and chopping steps in the frozen snow with their boots and climbing "staves," with rocks falling from the cliffs above, and imminent peril often counseling them to go back, it was a two-hour struggle to the top, a vertical distance, the writer estimated, of about 300 feet. His diary continues:

"At 3 o'clock we reached the summit of Mount Hood. Never in all my life have I seen a grander or more impressive sight....To the east we could trace the Columbia River, apparently, as far as Fort Walla Walla. We could see the Blue Mountains and the rolling prairies. To the north there were three snow-capped mountain peaks — St. Helens, Rainier and Adams. To the northwest we saw two lakes which have never been explored, and which have probably never been visited by a white man. They appear to be very deep and have high banks and are on a tableland at an elevation of about 7000 feet. (These probably are Bull Run and Lost lakes.)

"To the westward we could see Portland. With our telescopes we could even see the windows in the churches of Portland. We saw a smoke at Oregon City which we decided came from a foundry there. With our glasses we could see a cluster of houses marking the site of Salem. To the south we could see several snow-capped peaks. We counted five lakes of various sizes, shining like looking glasses. To the east rose the purple-blue range of the Blue Mountains while far to the west was the softened outline of the Coast range. Above us the sky was a deep Prussian blue. The north side of the mountain falls off almost perpendicularly.

"The four of us who reached the top were H. L. Pittock, Lyman Chittenden, Wilbur Cornell and myself.... We stuck our flagstaff on the extreme summit and the flag straightened out in the breeze. The four of us formed a circle around the flag and gave three cheers. Our feet were cold but our hands and faces were warm. Our descent was fully as dangerous but less wearisome than the climb to the summit. When we had passed the most dangerous place we sat down and slid, until one has done so it is hard to realize how far you go.

"Upon our arrival at our camp the effect of the trip soon began to be realized. Our hands and faces were scorched. That night we suffered excruciating pain and torture from our eyes. One of our party who made the summit was blind and the rest of us almost so. Our hands were chapped and our faces blistered. We spent the Sabbath in lamentations and groans. The reality of our suffering is far beyond my description. We camped there for some days as we were too much afflicted to travel. When we finally arrived in Portland some of our acquaintances did not recognize us, thinking we were Spaniards."

Mrs. Glenn thus failed by a short distance to be the first woman to climb the mountain. The first women made it 10 years later, in 1867 — Mary Robinson, who later became Mrs. W. F. Gilkey, and Fannie Case, who married F. H. Harvey.

The story of Dryer's Mount Hood attempt is told in the August 19 1854 edition of the *Weekly Oregonian*. Dryer wrote a rather droll account, with little of the viewpoint of the trained observer, and except for occasional sentences describing the terrain about the base of Mount Hood, it is difficult to identify his route. With

Captain O. Travaillot, a French mariner who quit the seas to become a merchant, he left Portland August 4 to meet enroute Wells Lake and "Captain" Barlow (actually William Barlow, son of the Mount Hood road builder) who was to be their guide. General Joel Palmer had been expected, but he did not show up.

Judge Cyrus Olney, of the Oregon Territorial bench, Major Granville O. Haller, Indian war figure of the army detachment at The Dalles, and a native guide were to meet them at the snowline on the south side of the mountain.

Dryer and his companions met Judge Olney, the major and the Indian apparently near White River canyon at timberline, probably not far from the site of Timberline lodge today. Because of a storm they dropped down some distance and camped. All had ridden horses to the mountain. On this same day, it is stated, they had explored from the south side far around to the northeast, quite high, seeking a route. They decided finally that the only way to the summit was "southeast by east" of the mountain. The party at sunset, Dryer narrates, saw "smoke" rising from the tip.

"It has not generally been supposed that Mount Hood at this time was volcanic," he wrote.

Next morning they rode the horses as high up the slopes as possible and left them in charge of Barlow. The members of the party had "creepers," ropes and "mountain staffs" shod with iron. Here is the reference showing the route of the summit attempt:

"We traversed a narrow ridge between the headwaters of Dog River on our right and a tributary of the De Chutes on our left."

Hood River at that time was called Dog River, and White River flows into the Deschutes. The great tongue of rock extending up the mountain to become finally Steel's cliff above the crater divides these basins. Dryer continues:

"The ridge was attained by crossing a chasm 500 feet deep formed by the water of the De Chutes branch."

This is the canyon of the White River below the glacier. The Indian trail lies up its west side. Proceeding up the ridge they found the snow in waves "like a chopped sea," lying very steeply, in which they had to dig steps. Haller and Travaillot, affected by the "rare" air, became dizzy and were forced to stop. Judge Olney dropped out on a pitch of "70.5 degrees by the theodolite."

"Finally at 2:30 pm. we attained the summit on the southeast side," it is stated. From this phrase, "on the southeast side," it is believed that Dryer only got to the top of Steel's cliff and did not persist in the stiff climbing required to gain the highest point, a considerable distance beyond. The top, Dryer described as being extremely narrow and lying in a crescent shape facing southwest. This is true of that part of the summit wall.

The main ridge, he went on, consisted of decomposed "volcanic substances" of light reddish color, with cones 20 to 50 feet high at intervals. Between these cones were numerous holes varying from the size of a water bucket to 2 or 3 inches. These openings were emitting "hot gas" with a "strong sulphuric odor." In passing along the ridge for nearly a half mile, many of these fumaroles were found, some hotter than others. He had no thermometer but hand tests indicated heat near the boiling point.

These characteristics are to be found along the ridge today. There is at least one fumarole still active there, and plenty of evidence of many more are shown by incrustations on the rocks. A novice in mountaineering terms might well have described the gendarmes and other formations along the rough ridges as "cones" and when the mountain top is bare in late season it has a light reddish cast. As for the heat of the fumaroles, recent research has shown some of those in the crater below to be 193 degrees F, the boiling point at that altitude, with others cooler.

That Dryer did not mention the great peaks to the north, the lakes and the Columbia River, by far the most striking objects of the view from the actual summit, is additional evidence that he did not go high enough to see them. They are not visible from Steel's cliff.

Descending, they found Travaillot, Haller and Olney making observations. They were unable to use a barometer loaned them by Peter Skene Ogden, then governor of the Hudson's Bay company at Vancouver, and Dryer describes a bit of scientific humbuggery based on tables and data devised by Baron Humboldt on the average thickness of mountain snow in different seasons and at varying elevations, and latitude an important factor. By these they determined the altitude of the peak at 18,361 feet — the "north pinnacle" highest. Among mountaineers it is a broad application of the term to call Mount Hood's summit ridge a pinnacle. Their base camp was computed to be at an elevation of 11,250 feet.

Dryer and his friends were subjected to a good deal of twitting about their Mount Hood exploit when they returned to Portland. Particularly ridiculed was their claim of having established the altitude at 18,361 feet. Dryer was irked by the comments, especially of the editors in Portland and in the Willamette Valley with whom he was warring constantly.

The point the Dryer party actually reached will never be known, but certainly their route was feasible. Will Langille demonstrated this 35 years later, when he took several groups that way to the summit. The passage is known today as the Wy'east Trail. Wy'east Trail and Langille's route were variations at lower elevations from the course that Dryer described, but high on the ridge they are identical.

Will Steel, in his cutting, denunciatory style of writing, was particularly savage in denouncing Dryer. He flatly asserted that it was impossible to climb the mountain over the ridge that today bears his name. Yet at the time he was writing, Langille had demonstrated that it could be done.

7.   Settlers of the Meadows

Government Camp, now a busy community at the south base of Mount Hood, has not always held this important position. In the early days of travel to the Willamette, it was a camping place because of the open meadows that lie between Mount Hood and Tom, Dick & Harry Mountain. To the first immigrants it was known as Camp Creek. The stream flowing past the settlement and across the meadows, then charging down Yocum Falls a couple of miles west, is still called Camp Creek.

Army records divulge the origin of the name Government Camp. When Lieutenant William Frost brought a government train to Oregon in October 1849 from Fort Leavenworth Kansas, he reached these meadows. Bad weather had set in and the Barlow road was in such state as to force Frost to store some of the wagons for the winter. From "the government camp in the mountains" the name stuck, although for years it was known as "the government camp on Camp Creek" before growing up to a capital letter title.

By far the more attractive camping spot and stopping place in the pass, at that time, was what we know now as Summit Meadows — earlier as Summit Prairie. This is open country lying southeast of the base of Multorpor Mountain. It was a spot which weary travelers welcomed when finally attained. Their first glimpse came as they reached Barlow Pass, after the long grind — nearly a dozen miles — uphill from the White River crossing. Once in Summit Meadows they were practically on top and past the real divide of the range. But a meandering road presented an uphill drag for another mile over the often boggy road, before heading down Laurel Hill on the last lap to the Willamette country.

Here they were at the base of the great peak they had first seen from the Blue Mountains many weeks before. To reach it, they had crossed harsh, arid country, beset by heat, dust and sandstorms. At Summit Prairie they felt the humid breeze of the western valley, carrying its touch of ocean balm, while icy streams rippled from the snowbanks above on that vast slope, extending continuously before them to the crest of the snowcap. It is no wonder that Summit Prairie is chronicled as a happy place to which, in after years, many of these very travelers returned for summer outings.

Among the stream of humanity at Summit Meadows in 1868 was a man who fell in love with the region so deeply that he remained there until the tragic end of his life. Little is known of the early years of Perry Vickers. He is believed to have fought in the Civil War and reputedly of "good family," for he was educated and aristocratic of mien, a splendid host but of fiery temper and quick with a gun. He had acquired considerable money from unknown source. After his death the land he occupied was dug over many times by treasure seekers, but no cache ever was found.

Vickers probably was the south side's most romantic figure. He was the first settler and guide. He gazed on the peak with the rhapsodic vision of a poet. He composed verse in the most classic form, with rhymes somewhat in the style of Tennyson. Inspiration for his compositions came from his wandering over the mountain. He was the pioneer example of those solitary roamers of forest and height today that we call "lone wolf" climbers. One of his chief contributions to knowledge of the peak lay in debunking the belief that temperatures on the summit at night sank to frightful depths that no man could survive.

By his own admission, Vickers came to Oregon under a cloud. He told Stephen Coalman that he had swum the Columbia River wearing leg irons as a fugitive from a Washington Territory prison and was a victim of persecution. As members of the same fraternal order Coalman and the others believed Vickers's story. He worked on the Barlow road and settled at Summit Prairie, where he built a cabin and began a trading business. He is remembered as one who never failed to help anybody in distress. When wagons broke down, or there was illness or other mishap on the trail, he would saddle his horse and ride out to give aid at any hour. He harvested the wild hay on the prairie, cured it and sold it, but to those in need who could not pay, he gave it without charge.

Vickers never attempted to obtain title to his land. He remained a squatter. After his death others moved in uncontested. One of these was Horace Campbell, known far and wide as "King David" because of his religious eccentricities. His brother Hector drove a stage. Horace rebuilt Vickers's Summit House and constructed an Indian teepee at the rear, with a central fireplace and a smoke hole at the peak. It stood as a landmark for many years. Some of the last of the wagon-train immigrants used this building for quarters.

Of all this activity there remains only a forlorn little cemetery. Two stones mark the graves of Perry Vickers and a two-month old baby, "son of W. and L. Barclay," who died at the Prairie in 1882. When Vickers lay dying of a bullet wound, his last words were to ask that they bury him next to the grave of the baby he had helped inter the year before.

The Vickers tragedy was the first known crime on Mount Hood. A man named Steele, who had worked at a ranch east of Gresham, stole a shotgun and fled to the mountain, and a justice of the peace pursued the fugitive. At Summit Meadows Vickers joined the mounted posse, and they soon reached the White River crossing. The group agreed to stalk the fugitive together but Vickers, seeing Steele by a campfire, charged on impulse. While he was dismounting, Steele fired. Vickers emptied a revolver after the fleeing Steele, then sank to the ground mortally wounded. They carried him into Cornelius Gray's cabin at the White River crossing where he died several hours later.

At Summit Prairie Vickers's friends cut down a tree at the springs (later called "Swim") and made a rough coffin. A niece erected the stone that is seen today. The Summit House, ravaged by time and vandals, disintegrated and finally disappeared.

In this same year also occurred the first tragedy suspected of being directly connected with the mountain's heights. Mount Hood was then a remote place with poor roads and no telephone, so news events often were fragmentary and long delayed in reporting.

Not much is known of a soldier named Bernhard who strayed from the camp at timberline and disappeared. He was from Vancouver, with a government supply party, and his officers felt he deserted, but Bernhard's friends doubted this. They believed he climbed to the snowfields and fell into a crevasse.

People who choose high mountains for their abode are individuals of strong, purposeful character and courage, else they do not remain long. There is a perpetual austerity about high peaks and an unbending majesty to which the mountain dweller must subscribe. Living alone becomes unbearable unless one has an acute awareness of the surroundings.

Oliver C. Yocum, the Government Camp pioneer, was one who established such an accord; William Gladstone Steel was another. Yocum might have been the most versatile person ever to live in Mount Hood country. His quick, intelligent mind made his existence there both easy and busy, despite the fact that for months on end he would see no other human face. No one knowing him would call O. C. Yocum a jack of all trades, yet his occupations were numerous in the course of a long, happy life.

In his youth Yocum was apprenticed to a saddle-maker, and late in life he boasted he could make pack-saddles "as good as any to be found in the Cascades." He clerked in stores in Yamhill county and studied law. He learned the photography craft and, in Portland, had a commercial photo studio until a lung ailment drove him to the outdoors. He became a proficient surveyor and worked with a party that measured the Columbia River from the Canadian border into the Okanagan country.

An assiduous student of chemistry as well, he manufactured the first photographic dry plates seen in Oregon. He was the first cameraman on the summit of Mount Hood. He studied pharmacy too, and when he retired from Government Camp he worked in the pharmacy of the North Pacific Dental College in Portland. As a youth Yocum was a Shakespeare enthusiast who memorized many of the dramas and played the tragedian role. In 1865, with a theatrical troupe he toured the rough mining camps then booming in Idaho. Again, he farmed and in the '70's was a successful grain buyer in the Willamette valley.

With all this Yocum spent 23 years at the base of Mount Hood.

He first saw Mount Hood at age 4, in 1847, when he and his parents passed over the Barlow road in a covered wagon. He first climbed the mountain July 16 1883, with a party from the faculty of Willamette University, in Salem. On that trip he lugged a ponderous 8-by-10 camera; with plates and other gear it weighed 50 pounds. His pictures from that occasion are still found in Oregon collections.

When Yocum first took up residence at Government Camp, Vickers charged $25 for guide service in climbing the peak. Yocum first guided without charge, but after 11 years he decided the effort was worth $5 a day.

Yocum and Will Steel, close friends, had homestead claims at Government Camp south of the present Loop highway. To save money they built a small log cabin straddling the boundary between their claims. Steel bunked on his side of the line, Yocum slept on his side, so each could meet the residential requirement. For years their cabin stood in the trees south of Government Camp.

Yocum platted a townsite and applied for a post office, with the name Government Camp. The postal authority disliked two-word names so he chose Pompeii, as appropriate for a city at the base of a volcano. That name was duly registered at Oregon City but it never caught on. In 1900 when he began work on his hotel, he had trouble hauling in materials. So he brought in a portable sawmill and made lumber from his own woods. The hotel investment cost him more than $23,000.

When at the top of his powers Yocum was intensely active. One night he took a party to his climbing camp and set off with them, before dawn, toward the summit. He left them at the top, hurried back to timberline, guided a second group to the summit, then brought down the first party. Early that afternoon he took still another party to the top, and brought down the whole drove just as darkness fell at timberline.

George Prosser often climbed the mountain as assistant guide with Yocum, who rewarded him with a small piece of land. There he built the first cottage, on the south side of the Loop highway where he lived for many years. Many of the south side residents, Prosser said, came from eastern Oregon. The Portland people found it more convenient to go to the north side, by train to Hood River and by stage up to Cloud Cap.

Prosser and his wife were ardent bicyclists. Wheeling clubs were popular in the '90's, and they found Mount Hood attractive. Many climbers went to Government Camp on bikes.

Under the vigorous leadership of Colonel W. W. Hawkins, a bicycle path from Portland to Government Camp was seriously discussed. Yocum began experimenting with local sand and cement, and promised to build the first seven miles west of Government Camp; the path was to be two feet wide through a clearing six feet wide, and guards would keep horsemen and livestock away. But nothing ever came of it.

Yocum said Government Camp and Mount Hood were the scene of his best life's work. At 69 he retired from guiding in favor of his protege, Elijah Coalman. Yocum was an inspiring guide, an eager observer of nature and a teacher. He imparted to hundreds the love of mountaineering. The great western ridge of the mountain, dividing the Sandy and Reid Glaciers, bears his name. So does the falls of Camp Creek, which he discovered.

Crater Lake is Will Steel's monument, but his name is perpetuated in the cliffs of the Mount Hood crater opposite Crater rock, on the east side. He was one of the early climbers, took part in organizing the Oregon Alpine Club in 1887, and became first president of the Mazama Club. He was a prolific writer on outdoor topics; his works are among the most valuable of our early mountain records.

The Oregon Alpine Club grew from a circle of young men who climbed together on various peaks and liked to meet and compare notes. They gathered in Portland at J. M. Breck Jr.'s drug store, where they stored equipment. On September 14 1887 they organized the club with Yocum as chairman pro tem, and laid out an ambitious program of scientific study of the northwest mountains. Another project was a natural history museum. The club's chief achievement was placing register boxes on the summits of major peaks to safeguard the records of climbers. Some of these lasted for years. The one placed atop Mount Jefferson was drilled through and through by lightning.

The Alpine Club did not impose a climbing qualification for membership, which angered Will Steel. He dropped support and the club died. He then worked with others to form the Mazamas.

8. The Mountain Illumined

With Civil War memories still bright, Fourth of July celebrations were grand affairs in the latter decades of the 19th Century. Portland made elaborate preparations, with civic committees at work long in advance. Night illumination of Mount Hood, as a climax to the fireworks display, had been talked of for years. Not until the Oregon Alpine Club was organized were any steps taken to stage such a spectacular affair.

When the Fourth of July committee was planning its work in 1873, Perry Vickers offered to illuminate the mountain on the holiday. His offer was tabled for two reasons: fear of the high cost vs. uncertain results, and the common belief in those days that a human could not live in the night air on the summit. Just to show the committee its error Vickers took blankets, telescope, provisions, thermometer and a quantity of magnesium wire to the summit. At 9:30 pm, while 25 persons of "unimpeachable veracity" watched at Summit Prairie, he touched off the magnesium — the white fire glared bright in 10 displays.

"And we may venture to hope," *The Oregonian* chided later, "that being now experimentally proven, those croakers will hush their opposing voices if ever the grand illumination of Mount Hood on the Fourth of July is again mooted."

Besides his flares, Vickers watched his thermometer. He reported the minimum was 28 degrees above zero. But he never enjoyed the laurels showered on those who staged the "grand illuminations" 15 years later, because of his untimely death.

High hopes the city would see Mount Hood in night illumination flamed in Portland hearts in July 1877. A party left town a few days before and, at the appointed time spectators flocked to the high places. At 10 pm they saw a brilliant light near the summit. This light did not subside, however. Instead, it rose higher and higher in the sky. Next day the *The Oregonian* explained it was the planet Mars, by coincidence rising at the expected hour east of the peak. The climbers were afraid to stay all night, so they left a 110 by 15-ft. flag planted in the highest snow, but it remained unseen from the city.

On July 4 1885, after days of experimenting with a device they felt sure of, a party of young men left the city amid showers of publicity. After climbing to the summit, George Breck and C. H. Gove crossed, in early afternoon, from Crater Rock to Illumination Rock (then described as "a large flat rock facing west") and set up their contraption. They placed the red fire and covered it to keep off the wind, then set two alarm clocks for 10 pm. To each clock hammer was attached a string connecting to a bottle of "a liquid preparation." When the hammer jerked the string it would upset the bottle and the fluid would start the fire.

Confident that thousands watching would see a great display, the pair started down. They had gone but a short distance when they heard a noise like avalanching rock. Looking back they saw a tremendous flash as their red fire ignited. A falling rock, the disappointed pair found, had hit the bottle and set off the illumination six hours early.

The Portland News of June 25 1887 said that Will Steel, then a famous mountaineer and writer, would lead a party to "the misty mountain top" on Friday next with 150 pounds of lycopodium powder for the Fourth of July illumination. This time Steel and a group from the Alpine club promised success. The celebration committee gave $75 for expenses. A heliographing set was taken along for the group to flash Portland from the mountain. A half-pound of red fire was set off on Willamette Heights as a trial, and viewers at Vancouver saw it. They felt certain that burning 100 pounds would be seen at Portland from the mountain.

Great was the excitement at Portland. C. G. Glass, an army signal officer, was posted in the cupola of the customs house, equipped with telescope and heliographing device to return signals from the mountain. He combed the mountain from timberline to summit with his glass but, said the *The Oregonian*, "nary a flash was seen." Still the *News* that day was confident that illumination would occur and "...thus will the Fourth of July be fittingly terminated by one of the grandest displays imaginable."

"The experiment," headlined the *The Oregonian* next morning, of painting the summit red was a complete success." Thousands on "the bridge," on wharves, roofs, boats and the hills west of town saw the crimson glare above the clouds promptly at 11:30 pm — lasting 58 seconds. This, the paper said, "...was the most novel and highest illumination ever made, and was seen the farthest."

Three days passed before the party could return to Portland with news of their performance. In two spring wagons nine men, including drivers, had left the week before. They camped at Cherryville the first night, paid toll at the gate next morning and went up Laurel hill by the "new road" which was filled with snow in the canyon. All had to get out and push as the jaded horses floundered through the drifts. When they reached Government Camp they abandoned the wagons, packed equipment on two of the horses and started for timberline. But they had no pack saddles so the loads kept slipping as the horses skidded in the snowdrifts. They finally divided the burden among the men and sent the horses back.

They made camp in the forest. At this point in the account of the trip appears a statement that would curl the hair of any forest ranger today. As now, trees of the upper forest were draped with moss, so "before turning in for the night a number of them were fired, producing a startling and magnificent effect. Flames ran up the burning trees with wonderful rapidity, rushing skyward in a fiery column 50 feet above the tree tops."

This, it might be noted here, is an excellent description of those forest conflagrations we now call crown fires, the most dangerous and the worst to control. Under our stern laws now, these patriots of the 19th Century would have faced prison terms.

Early next morning a portion of the red fire and equipment was loaded on a toboggan and dragged through the forest. The snow lay in hummocks, with deep depressions around the trees. The party encountered great trouble and the procession finally halted while C. H. Gove went back for a horse. They lunched on canned Boston brown bread and "a nauseating concoction of beef tea, made by mixing the extract with snow and melting that in tin cups, a mixture that tasted of smoke and anything but beef." It was evident now that the attached *The Oregonian* reporter was tired of the project.

When the horse arrived at last and dragged the sled well above timberline, they made camp on a rocky island in the snow. That afternoon Steel tried to respond to the heliograph signals he received from Portland, but his apparatus was broken. Icy wind swept the camp, the reporter felt he himself "was probably the sickest one in camp." They had no fire and stopped eating the "canned beef and ship's bread that constituted the menu."

It must have been a scene of rare gloom. The sunset picture was "feebly appreciated," and "sunrise on the Fourth was below our expectations." The reporter asserted "sublimity is out of the market when men are chilled through and have nothing to eat but canned meat and ship's bread." Finally everyone got under way, lugging the red fire and extra clothes for Steel and Dr. J. M. Keene, who would stay on the mountain for the illumination. That frigid camp probably was high on Triangle moraine, for upon starting next morning the party was near the east base of Crater Rock and they climbed northwest to the pinnacle which, because of their exploit, henceforth became known as Illumination Rock.

At the base of the great western wall the red fire was laid, and all but Steel and Keene turned back. In late afternoon the loads were piled on the horse and soon the party reached Government Camp. Although tired and sunburned, the men sat up for the illumination. They were rewarded with a grand spectacle of a rosy glare over the whole mountainside, with every crag of the great crater wall set out, and tints on the surrounding hills.

So great was this success, and so wide was the publicity for Portland across the nation, that there could be no question about the illumination the next year. It was, in fact, "still greater and better." The pioneers had learned by their bitter experience of 1887, for the same *The Oregonian* reporter in 1888 wrote: "Last year the party lived on hardtack and snow, and there was a great deal more snow than hardtack. They will have boiled ham, bacon, flour, yeast powder, condensed milk and coffee, to say nothing of the demijohn of brandy and plenty of fishing tackle and shooting irons."

Lieutenant J. P. O'Neil, a Vancouver Barracks signal officer, accompanied the party this time, and his commander agreed to fire 13 mortar shells if he saw the illumination. Steel headed the party of 14 men, including Dr. Keene, Yocum, Gove, and J. M. Breck Jr. They had a signal station opened on the Kamm building in Portland, and the party was to signal its nightly progress with rockets. The party had a large government freight wagon this time, drawn by four army mules, and a two-horse express wagon, with one man on horseback.

Three days of storm blanketed the Northwest prior to the Fourth that year. The wagons got as far as timberline where the bivouac was dubbed "Camp Rain." Mount Hood was hidden from Portland by clouds, and no signals were observed. The mules pulled the toboggan and 120 pounds of red fire and other supplies for a short distance, but the animals soon began breaking through the snow. Eight men then towed the sled and three carried the ladder to be used for crossing the big crevasse, as this party intended to go to the summit. Near Crater Rock a severe storm broke, the snow froze, Dr. Keene and Steel nearly lost their lives in a slide. With everyone sheathed in ice in the driving sleet, the party was forced to turn back.

The storm continued the next day and the red fire was cached on the slope. That night Joseph Wilson and Will Langille arrived after a hike around the mountain from the north side. Langille, who later would become a celebrated guide on the north side, made his first ascent of Mount Hood the next day.

Better weather rewarded the intrepid group on the morning of the Fourth, and 11 finally reached Crater Rock. Wilson, Steel, Langille, Dr. Keene, E. D. DeWert and Gove went on to the summit. Professor W. A. Wetzel climbed to the top of Crater Rock.

The fire, laid in a pile 10 feet long, was ignited by Steel and Dr. Keene, who froze his feet slightly while waiting until 11 pm. Too fully occupied that day for the extra distance to Illumination Rock, they placed the fire near the base of Crater Rock. The clouds lifted in time for "nine-tenths of the population of Portland to see the display," which lasted more than two minutes.

9. North Side Pioneers

In its most majestic aspect Mount Hood dominates the beautiful valley of the river given its name. The mountain slopes are the source of water that feeds the lush orchards for which Hood River is known everywhere. Lofty peaks form the walls of the valley. The view southward from the Columbia River centers on a V where these meet, below the old volcano rising steeply to its crest.

The thought of making the mountain more accessible for recreation must have occurred to the first residents of this valley. It crystallized in 1883 when preliminary explorations for an approach to the slopes were made by Captain Henry C. Coe, James Graham, Oscar L. Stranahan, whose family name is on the ridge east of the upper valley, and David R. Cooper, of Cooper's Spur fame. They had in mind establishing a tourist resort.

Beyond the Middle Fork crossing (still called the Toll Bridge) there were no roads. From there to timberline the land was wilderness, partially open in spots but covered for the most part with almost impenetrable forest and brush. The party started in dry summer weather and a fire preceded them, burning out the trees and undergrowth almost to the Elk Beds, 5 miles north of the site of Cloud Cap Inn. Roaring Camp, at a spring on the ridge north of the Mount Hood Lodge site, was so named because of the sound of this blaze. As the only known water along the route, the spring was the base campsite during the construction period and a watering place for stock used in transportation.

Not far from the site of the present American Legion camp

and the forest guard station at Tilly Jane Creek, in the gully below Cloud Cap Inn, Mrs. David Cooper became hostess at a tent camp. Mrs. Cooper thus was the first to operate a season-long public resort at timberline on Mount Hood. A dining tent was erected, plus one for cooking, and more as required for housing patrons. Altogether it was a simple establishment but praised for abounding hospitality. People then were content with the facilities which enabled them to step so easily to the snows of Mount Hood.

The Coopers were natives of Scotland. Their children lived at the camp much of the time and helped by supplying trout and venison to the fare. The resort was maintained until the end of the 1889 season. Dave Cooper, the elder, was the first guide for the glaciers and lower slopes. He climbed the long ridge, named for him, between Eliot and Newton Clark Glaciers and extending from timberline two-thirds of the way to the summit. Bert Stranahan, stage driver and horseman of the old school, piloted the wagon and patrons through the bridgeless stream and up the road.

Among the earliest visitors, Dr. Thomas Lamb Eliot, a Portland Unitarian minister, took inspiration from the mountain and spread news of its wonders far afield. The associations of Dr. Eliot, pioneer leader of his faith in the west, were chiefly with the north side and the Hood River valley. He enjoyed rough camping with Professor Louis F. Henderson, a botanist. Dr. Eliot ascended Mount Adams in 1878.

In August 1880 Dr. Eliot, his brothers Christopher and Edward, joined Professor Henderson and E. L. Smith and Newton Clark of Hood River, and 6 others. They set out from Hood River to find a lake that had been seen from Mount Hood but was unknown. They found this body of water in deep forest on August 21. At Dr. Eliot's suggestion it was named Lost Lake.

Dr. Eliot is credited with naming Cooper's Spur and Coe Glacier. In a formal ceremony at the mountain, August 8, 1888, Dr. Eliot christened the east side glacier for his friend Newton Clark, who had made the initial ascent over the north side route. E. L. Smith named the great north side glacier for Eliot.

Professor Henderson combed the region searching for new plants. Dr. and Mrs. Perry Barrett, Hood River pioneers, explored the lovely Eden Park beside Cathedral Ridge long before it was rediscovered by hikers of the 1920's. Barrett Spur, the high cockscomb rock between Ladd and Coe Glaciers, perpetuates their name.

Newton Clark, a civil engineer who homesteaded near Hood River among the first settlers, surveyed much of the land about Mount Hood. It is fitting that a glacier bears his name because of his notable exploration of slopes that were believed unscalable.

Early on August 11 1887 eight men left the Cooper camp and filed in upward traverse over Eliot Glacier, then on Coe above Barrett Spur. They rounded Pulpit Rock and began to ascend along its westerly flank. After what was described as "bad climbing on slippery steep talus," five men gave up. Clark, William J. Smith and Elmer Rand went on, attaining Cathedral Ridge high up and proceeding to the top. They carried a heliograph, intending to signal Hood River, but found the air too smoky.

"This probably will be the last climb for the north side for some time," wrote one man. "It is no climb for tourists."

Small boys of the upper valley were glad to see A. J. Johnson, a commercial florist from Astoria, on his visits to the north side, because he paid well for gathering conifer seeds and Mount Hood lily bulbs for shipment to European markets.

Mrs. David Cooper, alone at the camp with her children in the summer of 1886, worried over forest fires raging in the upper valley. One afternoon high winds fanned the flames in sudden fury up the Middle Fork canyon. Enveloped in dense smoke and with flaming brands falling about, Mrs. Cooper snatched a few necessities and led her little band up the canyon to the glacier. She remained there until the fire abated. The flames swept to the top of the eminence where Cloud Cap now stands, leaving the whitened snags that gave the crest the name Ghost Ridge.

When they had time, Mrs. Cooper and her children climbed to that ridge. With never lessening pleasure they scanned the sheer north face of the peak, and shuddered as avalanches roared down into the cirque of Eliot Glacier.

The winter of 1889-89 saw little snow in the Cascades, and in March a team and wagon went almost to timberline. That spring the Mount Hood Trail and Wagon Road Company was sold to William M. Ladd, banker, and C. E. S. Wood, attorney, of Portland and renamed Mount Hood Stage Company. They immediately began improvements. A crew cleared the right of way, followed by a gang of Chinese laborers who did the grading by hand.

This use of Chinese labor placed two names still memorable in the upper valley. "China Fill," anathema to motorists for many years, was a place below Cloud Cap on the road — a grade of 22 per cent on a sharp curve built over a small gulch. Few cars could overcome it. Again, "China Hill" was a stretch of road below Mount Hood Lodge.

At the site of the old ford a bridge was constructed over the East Fork, minor streams were spanned, grades cut down and a stage station and barn were built at the spring. When these labors had progressed enough for a mountain camp, they built Cloud Cap Inn. From a stand of the amabilis fir, some 2-1/2 miles below Cloud Cap, logs were hewn, drawn to the site by teams and bolted together. They built two huge fireplaces from rock of the nearby cliffs, piped water 1200 feet from a spring in the Tilly Jane draw, installed ranges, baths and good beds. Then, with comfortable chairs scattered about, Cloud Cap Inn opened for business at 5837 feet above sea level.

The Inn construction job was well done on an arete exposed to the fury of the mountain gales. It is still serviceable, with water flowing through the pipes laid in 1889. This project rivaled the Union Pacific railroad as a major one in the valley.

Cloud Cap Inn was designed by William Marcy Whidden, Portland architect; John Hamilton, also of Portland, superintended the work with James L. Langille in charge of construction. Thomas McKay, a railroad builder, brought in Chinese labor gangs. Lewis H. Adams, of Portland, bought the stage stock and took charge of transportation.

Lewis Adams and his wife managed the Inn when it opened in August 1889. The first patrons were 6 members of a coaching party, guests of the late Malcolm Moody, The Dalles, who arrived with his own rig and four, on August 6. A few weeks later the Inn closed for the winter.

That winter saw extreme weather, with deep snows and severe storms. Many feared the Inn would blow away or be crushed under the weight of snowdrifts. To see how it fared, Will and

H. D. Langille set out for a visit in February 1890. They traveled on home-made skis — the first skiing trip in winter on the north side. They reached Elk Beds cabin the first day, and the Inn the next, and found it in bright sunshine with water dripping from the eaves. The building was unharmed. Thereby they dispelled the myth that winter weather at timberline could not be endured. [*One hundred years later the building still stands.*]

Adams, the Langilles, the photographer A. B. McAlpin and Theodore Dallas, carrying an 18 by 22 plate camera, went to the Inn in March to record and photograph winter scenes. The success of these trips enticed others to go, and in time they grew popular. Still, they could not open the Inn that year until July 12 as snow-drifts blocked the road.

An open coach and four met the Portland train at Hood River about noon each and and left at once for the Inn. The first relay was of 10 miles to the Joe Divers ranch, on the Little Luckamas Creek. After lunch the rig proceeded with fresh horses to the Elk Beds. Here Dallas had six range horses harnessed and waiting for the dusty grind on up the mountain. The departure was described as something of a runaway, with the coach swaying precariously. Soon the horses expended their energy and settled to the effort on the steep ascent. The Inn was reached in time for dinner, 5-1/2 to 6 hours from the railway.

Although the Inn — costing its owners upwards of $50,000 — was extensively advertised, only 88 guests registered that season. The Inn had been intended as a unique, high-class establishment and it was so conducted, but it was ahead of the times and the poor patronage ran up increasing deficits. In this uncertain situation, the owners had little hope for the future. They sold the transportation stock and indicated the Inn was to be closed indefinitely at the end of the 1890 season.

10. In Tantsana's Regime

For many years the Langille family was identified with activities on the north side and the Hood River valley. They left Nova Scotia in 1880 and settled on a ranch 13 miles from Hood River in 1883. They moved into the Cloud Cap picture for its most lively period, in 1891, when Mrs. James L. Langille, mother of Will and Douglas, took charge. The elaborate establishment of the previous year was trimmed down and stage service reduced to actual needs.

The affectionate name of Tantsana was given Mrs. Langille by her sons as the family read the book *Story Of An African Farm* so popular at the time. She was also called the Lady of the Mountain. Cloud Cap in her day was described as the most pleasant Alpine inn in North America, and her tact and warm hospitality contributed much in making it so.

Will and Douglas were at the Inn most of the time, both men of all work, but Will did more of the trail guiding. Both were familiar with the summit long before they went to Cloud Cap. Will's first climb was made over the south side route in Steel's second illumination expedition of July 4 1888.

The Langille brothers must have made the initial climb over the Steel's cliff route to the summit, unless one credits Dryer's claims of 1854. Approached from either the south or north side, this route in recent years has been called the Wy'east Trail by members of that club of mountaineers who have done much to develop and popularize it.

The present Wy'east route includes the ascent of a chimney

directly from the ice at the head of Newton Clark Glacier to gain access to the top of the cliff. The chimneys are cracks or narrow channels worn by erosion down the cliff faces. Rock fragments bouncing down these dents endanger climbers.

The Langilles apparently did not use the chimney but traversed the glacier to its southern moraine, then scrambled up the nose of the ridge from the point where more solid rock begins. In 1889 Will Langille and his father, James; Erskine Wood, son of C. E. S. Wood; Herbert Nichols, and Will Sayre attained the top of the cliff but were unable to press on to the summit.

The following year, with Lewis H. Adams and A. B. McAlpin the photographer, Will Langille went along the rim to its highest point. They used a rope on the more dangerous chimney in the last 200 feet of elevation. Once on top they celebrated with a bottle of champagne.

With a party from the Inn, Langille was on the cliff again in 1891. The party included Anne Lang of The Dalles, Horatio Green of Portland, Fred Josselyn and Will Smith. They were approaching a particularly difficult gully, whose trough extended almost perpendicular to the glacier 1500 feet below. Langille cut off a 12-foot section of their 200-foot climbing rope and tied Lang and Josselyn together. He then crawled around the gully to a good anchorage on the other side, and told them to cross by clinging to the big hand line which was between him and Green.

Josselyn was ahead and both were between the cliff and the line when Lang's foot gave way. She pitched forward, striking Josselyn who toppled and threw her up on the outside of the hand line. In an instant the two were dangling over the dizzy chute — Lang head downward, the rope that tied them together being over the other strand. This saved them from going down to the glacier, but it left them dangling 25 feet below the rest of the party on a ledge, swinging clear from the wall, as the hand line was new and not as tight as it should have been.

Langille had a firm anchorage, while Green was backed up by Smith. Josselyn was able to get his footing and, after considerable effort the two were drawn up safely. The climb, although the summit was a short distance away, was abandoned there. It is said that none except Anne Lang cared to go on.

Will and Douglas Langille also were the first to ascend the Cooper's Spur route. They had looked at it many times, as had other climbers, but the avalanching and that bulge of rock near the top seemed impressively forbidding, while the higher snow slopes were of terrifying steepness. To Will the route never appeared impossible but he yielded to the opinion of others. Too, he had often looked down on it from the summit, a point of view very discouraging to climbers who have never seen it from any other aspect. The Langilles had been taking summit parties the longer way around to Steel's cliff for several years. On July 5 1893 they gave the Spur and the northeast face another good looking over and decided to tackle it.

Will then was using an ice ax modeled after the beautifully-wrought creations of the Swiss, forged by a Portland blacksmith. He needed it badly that day when, just a few feet from their goal, they confronted an overhanging comb of ice and frozen snow; it was blown out by the southerly storms that roar over the summit in winter, and lies at an angle as abrupt as any to be found on Mount Hood. Up there at the very tip where the incline so approaches the perpendicular that one has to lean out to see the snow face a few feet below, the brothers clung for interminable time while Will hacked away gingerly, chopping steps in the overhang above his head. Douglas complained that his feet were frozen but then he stepped on the top in triumph. The two had opened a new route, destined to become increasingly popular and to know the tread of thousands in future.

They re-ascended the route several times that summer, and the next year it was followed often. The trail was made easier by hanging a thousand feet of 5/8-inch lifeline from a knob of rock that protruded from the snow 75 feet below the rim. It was difficult at that time to find an anchorage on the top.

On July 19 1894 Douglas Langille piloted a large party that traversed the north side to the summit where the Mazama Club was organized. Will was ill at the time.

Will Langille also made a solo climb over approximately the same route that 30 years later was known as the Sunshine Trail. This one courses westward across Eliot and Coe Glaciers to Horseshoe Rock, thence over Cathedral Ridge to the summit. He found the snow above Coe too steep for a return alone so he made his way back to the Inn over the Spur.

The first recorded death of a Mount Hood climber was Frederic Kirn, an elderly Portland grocer of Swiss descent. In July 1896 he was carried by an avalanche above Cooper's Spur over a wall on the east side. The body came to rest within a few feet of a deep crevasse near the upper bergschrund of Newton Clark Glacier.

Kirn arrived at Cloud Cap Inn after walking up from Hood River, and inquired about the route. He declined guide services after examining the trail; he said he had climbed in the Alps. Early next morning, after fortifying himself with a cup of coffee, he set out while Tantsana watched with a telescope, as she often did with climbing guests. Late that afternoon she raised the alarm when she could not see Kirn's tracks in the snow above the rocks. At 5:30 Will Langille went to find him.

Kirn's tracks were easy to follow. About 700 feet below the top Will found his steps veered eastward from the regular route, through steep terrain always avoided because of avalanche risk. When Will saw evidence of a new slide across Kirn's tracks he knew the worst — it rode over a sharp bluff above Newton Clark. Working down with caution, he was able to see the body where it had fallen unimpeded many hundreds of feet to the boulder-strewn ice far below. He returned to the Inn.

Langille and five others crossed the Spur next morning much lower down and climbed the glacier to retrieve the body. With difficulty they inched down the steep, icy slope, but by evening Kirn's body was lashed to a horse and taken to the Inn.

Before he left to follow the the gold rush in Alaska in 1897 Will Langille had made 50 ascents and in his last seven days at the Inn he escorted seven parties to the summit. He quit with the achievement that all guides seek — no accidents. In the days of the Langille brothers the Spur route was made "foolproof," so far as their own parties were concerned. The trail was always roped carefully with substantial lifelines, and the avalanche lanes of the head wall were avoided. Climbers not only had the lifelines, they were roped together.

Douglas Langille continued guiding through 1899, completing an even 100 ascents. He Joined the U. S. Geological Survey under

Henry Gannett, the geographer.

One of the saddest things that can happen to climbers on snow-clad peaks is snowburn. Even under clouds this occurs, for the sun's rays penetrate the vaporous blanket in the sky to reflect with devastating effect on the exposed skin of the mountaineer. One needs only look at a flaming face and realize it will be a mass of blisters next day, and what torture can be prevented with protective measures. Heavy veils once were the vogue but they were hot and obscured vision too much. The mixture applied to the skin most often by early climbers was charcoal and a heavy coat of vaseline so it would wipe off easily. This was the precaution of the Langilles.

Theatrical grease paint, applied over cold cream, was a later innovation. Coal-black faces with white rings around the eyes where goggles gave the necessary protection, are often seen in the pictures of proud "summit parties" before the turn of the Century. Alpenstocks carried by climbers were sturdy, but homemade. Ordinary screws in the soles of boots, or the triangle plates one sees on baseball shoes, were the casual climbers' stock armor against slipping. It was obvious from earliest days that horses could be taken up on Cooper's Spur, and they were so used before the Langilles took over the Inn.

Enthusiastic accounts of climbs with the Langilles are numerous in the printed record of that day. Train-ride in the Columbia Gorge…the stage with spirited teams at Hood River… luncheon at Toll Bridge…the cooling spring at the Elk Beds after the dusty highway ride…the vast panorama at Cloud Cap of mountains great and small, forests west and the plains of central Oregon to the east…the charm that Tantsana seemed to cast on everyone…gay parties around the huge fireplaces…and the unforgettable climbs. Oregon holds no more delightful lore than these stories about Cloud Cap.

One mountain climb in a lifetime fulfills both the curiosity and ambition of a great many of us. The Langilles knew this well and recognized the achievement with certain ritual. As soon as Will or Douglas had cached their ropes at the edge of the snow line for the next party to come, and everyone had gone to the Inn, the successful ones were allowed to go to the register and — very solemnly — sign the word "Summit" by their names.

This done, a tack was pierced through the climber's personal card, a silver dollar placed against the card, and the whole business tossed carefully against the beams of the ceiling. The dollar was the hammer expected to drive the tack into the wood and impale the card for future visitors to see.

Langille Crags, the pinnacled wedge of rocks that extends along the west side of Eliot Glacier, not far from the Inn, were of course named for this family. From their topmost point Douglas Langille stood in June 1924 and scattered the ashes of his mother, Tantsana, to be carried by the everlasting wind over the snow fields and the ice she had scanned vigilantly for the safety and happiness of many guests.

11. Autos Make The Grade

One would never suspect that Horace Mecklem, Portland business executive, civic worker and member of the school board, had begun his career in the west as a "mountain man." That was the case, however, and Cloud Cap Inn was the scene of these early events. Mrs. Langille was his aunt and after arriving in the west he spent the seasons of 1901 and 1902 in her employ.

In 1905 the Mecklems were married at Waugwingwin, the inn that stood those days on the site of the present Columbia Gorge Hotel, just west of Hood River. They went immediately to Cloud Cap for the summer. Mecklem was the man-of-all work, keeping books, waiting tables in the dining room, cutting wood, helping on the mountain, occasionally guiding, and after the Langilles retired in 1906, he ran the Inn.

In North Side history 1905 was a blue ribbon year, and in Mecklem's belief, one of the best from a standpoint of prosperity the Inn ever enjoyed. Motor stage service was instituted; for the first time an automobile was driven to the very door.

Two cars started on that momentous expedition up the valley, and as the chugging monsters drilled along the roads, horses broke in terror. H. M. Covey, one of Portland's first car dealers, drove the sturdy Cadillac "one lunger" that surmounted every difficulty to knock at the door of the Inn. Old timers will recall these blue-nosed high tonneaued cars with a rear door. And they were enduring; the funny old "one lungers" were to be seen in service as late as the First World War, far outmoded as to style and mechanics, but still stoutly performing their errands.

Mecklem drove the other car, a Pierce-Arrow, one of the first in Portland. It was owned originally by the Failing sisters. Without chains on the wheels it was in difficulty as soon as it encountered steep grades, and on the notorious China Fill its wheels bogged down in the volcanic ash of the road.

Covey drove back the following morning, and it is of record that appearance of the unmuffled "Cad" caused seven runaways, with angry ranchers shouting they would lynch the driver if he ever came that way again.

While the rugged Cadillac was the first car to surmount those heights there is a capital story told by Fay Fuller, the Mazamas' early historian, about the initial attempt by automobiles to go to Cloud Cap.

The year was 1901, the car's owner was E. Y. Judd, of Pendleton, and the machine, with three cylinders, was hailed as the only gasoline-propelled car on the Pacific coast. Its motor generated 12 horsepower and its maximum speed was 18 miles an hour. Extra supplies of fuel were hauled to stations along the route. On the morning in July when the great adventure started, a team and wagon went ahead with the baggage and another followed to aid in case of trouble. Two equestrians also were in the procession to "allay the fright of refractory animals," namely snorting farm horses that had never seen such a thing before.

The third cylinder quit 12 miles out of Hood River, but finally was restored to action and after a tremendous tussle the car got up Booth Hill with the driver steering while walking alongside. The water pump gave up after the car had descended a "rattling good grade" at 20 miles an hour, and finally the effort was abandoned not far from the Elk Beds. Judd and his party were taken in a horse-drawn rig the rest of the way where Tantsana, ever resourceful, consoled the motorist with the remark that snow alone had stopped him from getting through. A "strong team" was just behind next day in case of another breakdown but the car reached Hood River without further incident.

The Pierce went into regular stage service, but never got above the Fill, and a turnaround was established 3 miles below the Inn, with horse-drawn rigs carrying passengers the rest of the way. William Edick, later sheriff of Hood River County, drove the stage at the upper end of the load. His vehicle was a 3-seated hack, with 4 steeds for motive power. He scoffed at Mecklem's announcement that cars would make the grade that summer, but they did, and live horsepower on the pull soon was superseded by the energy from gasoline combustion.

Advent of the motor stage, reducing time for the journey from Hood River to 3 hours from 8, brought many patrons to the Inn in 1907. Among the passengers going up in the first autos were Malcolm Moody and the Lang girls of The Dalles.

Automobiles were somewhat later in coming to the south side. This was due largely to the lack of good roads east of Sandy. But they came, and served eventually to outdo development of resorts on the north slopes.

Lije Coalman was a foreman in a hilarious attempt of 1916 to drive an automobile up to Crater Rock. In those days motor makers believed stunts were necessary part of publicity to sell cars, and they tried to outdo each other in newer, bigger enterprises. This costly adventure was undertaken in utmost seriousness but the public that was supposed to be impressed never saw it that way.

From Portland the car was driven up Laurel hill in May, finally halting in deep snow, and Coalman and 13 huskies took over. Three sets of cleated tracks were used from that point, the idea being to carry these sections of portable road around in front of the car as it advanced. Three weeks passed in making a couple of miles to Government Camp. Of course this was the first car at the Camp in 1916 — itself an achievement. That particular competition was keen when there was no thought of keeping a winter road open to the mountain.

From Government Camp Coalman and his men turned up the old road to timberline, relaying their portable "highway," often shoving the car and sometimes shoveling a path through drifts as the motor chugged industriously. After weeks of this — lasting well into June — the car finally reached a slope too steep near the base of Triangle Moraine, at an elevation of about 8000 feet. In triumph it was photographed with its nose pointing at the summit, and the return trip began. It was easier, of course, getting back to timberline, and by the time the party was well down in the forest the seasonal thawing of snow had advanced so far that the wooden tracks were abandoned. Whitened and warped by the weathering of passing seasons, they lay there beside the road for years, marking the invasion of Mount Hood by the ubiquitous automobile.

12. Mazamas and the Mountain

For almost a century the names Mazama and Mount Hood have been synonymous. The Mazama Club was organized on the summit July 19 1894 as a mountaineering society, the first of its kind on the Pacific Coast. Since then the name has become famous in the annals of high mountain exploration. The club library has the most complete record to be found of any single mountain.

The Mazamas' active program has taken members to almost every mountain center of western North America. From Lassen Peak and Mount Shasta in the south to Garibaldi Park and the Canadian Rockies in the north, their parties have camped. From the far western group of snow peaks in the Olympic peninsula to the Teton range in Wyoming their climbers have been in action. Each year the club holds a two-week outing in some mountainous region.

Mount Hood and the other "guardians" — Mount Jefferson, Three Sisters, Mount Rainier and Mount Baker — have been visited often and the library contains data on almost every physical subject pertaining to them. The club's contribution to science as it relates to Mount Hood is of impressive volume and value. It has been active in the conservation of forests and our most beautiful scenic regions. Its members have worked to keep the forests green, the camp sites clean and the trails open. In this the club has cooperated with the United States Forest Service and has seen many of its practices become regulations for the public.

In 1894 conditions for mountaineering were more arduous

than they are today. There were few trails and practically no roads to the high peaks. The activity was truly an invasion of the wilderness. Whenever wheeled transport was possible it was done with horse and wagon. Mountaineers of that time often had trouble getting pack horses for their equipment and supplies, and the animals had to be driven many miles before they could be used. A journey to any of the Cascade peaks took two to four days, so a two-week outing permitted little more than a week of climbing and hiking. As the years passed the Mazamas found many lovers of the outdoors following their pioneering steps into the hills. Government administration of these regions became more complete. Gradually trails were built, then came better roads and finally splendid highways to most of the mountains.

McNeil writes of prevailing conditions as he knew them in 1937. His "splendid highways" meant paved 2-lane roads, with steep grades and sharp curves, replacing rough gravel or dirt mountain paths. Greatly improved highways and cars have featured the half-century since then, along with better clothing and equipment for outdoor sports, and increased activity on the mountain. That growth, in turn, generated recreation facilities and accomodations, as well as a role of greater importance for the Mazamas.

When the Oregon Alpine Club broke up, Steel and a few others continued pressing for an organization composed of climbers, with qualifications which would insure this type of membership. They held first discussions in the summer of 1893 and a meeting that winter. It was attended by C. H. Sholes, J. Francis Drake, Francis C. Little, Martin W. Gorman, the botanist, and Steel. The group issued invitations for March 19 1894 to consider "a plan for organizing a mountain climbers' club, on the summit of Mount Hood, and spreading a banquet at the same time." About 40 attended and committees were formed. Soon afterward went forth the widely published call for the famous assault on the summit on July 19 1894. It was announced that the name of the group would be "Mazamas" — that the mazama is the American representative of the European chamois. They said the animal commonly known as the mountain goat, admittedly the best Alpinist in the country, was to be found in the mountains of the Pacific Coast. Those wishing to climb were advised to go either to Government Camp by team from Portland, The Dalles, or other point; or to Cloud Cap Inn by stage from Hood River.

The call further stated that an old-fashioned bean bake would be given Tuesday July 17 at Government Camp, a free-for-all. The following day the camp would be moved to timberline in time to "see the sunset on the Pacific Ocean, 100 miles distant." It was signed by Steel, Jennie Montague, G. D. Ames, the Langille brothers, and Malcolm A. Moody.

At his Government Camp homestead, Steel was standing in the meadows gazing at the peak. He was pondering a plan which would limit membership to those who were climbers and wanted affiliation because of their love of mountains. There came to him the idea of limiting this to those attaining the tops of peaks which bore on their flanks at least one living glacier and could be ascended only on foot. This qualification remains as the membership rule of the club today.

To Fay Fuller, the historian, fell the honor of relating in the annual publication the story of that first climb. The evening of July 17 found nearly 300 people in Steel's Meadow. A lesser number camped at Cloud Cap. By wagon and horseback the various groups had traveled over the poor road through the Sandy River valley. Some went by Adolph Aschoff's homestead at Marmot, on the north bank of the Sandy.

The next day the throng at Government Camp moved to timberline, where they "camped on such of the moraines as afforded good shelter from the winds." And, Fuller added, "at sunset many caught a glimpse of the Pacific Ocean, 100 miles distant." This last was based, no doubt, on good imagination by some of the enthusiasts — it has been established by investigators of a later day that the ocean is not visible from the summit.

Fuller's account continues: "Before 3 o'clock on the morning of the 19th, many had begun to climb, and by 7 o'clock the earlier climbers had reached Crater Rock, 1000 feet below the summit, while between 200 and 300 were far on their way. But by this time a storm, which had been gathering during the night, broke over the summit and came down upon the climbers. There was furious snow mixed with hail; while the piercing cold wind blew so strong as to make it necessary to hug rocks closely to escape being blown away. The storm lasted only about half an hour, but in that time nearly 100 turned back, considering the ascent hopeless for the day. More persevered, however, and soon after 8 o'clock the first party had reached the summit. From then until 2:30 straggling parties kept reaching the summit, on which there were at one time more than 50 persons. It was so uncomfortable there, however, that the greater number remained a short time, then returned to camp.

"Those who stayed on the summit had for some hours been observing the progress of a party from Cloud Cap Inn who were ascending the north side, but whom the storm had deterred from starting until 9 o'clock. This party reached the summit at 3 o'clock and the 40 or more then present proceeded immediately to organize the society as proposed, all huddling together on the one sheltered ledge which the summit afforded."

(The sheltered ledge was Mazama Rock, on the north side of the summit ridge, a precipitous formation so unstable that much of it has fallen away since then. It is shunned by climbers, who fear the whole mass may go tumbling a thousand feet down the head of Eliot Glacier.)

"Rev. Earl M. Wilbur acted as temporary chairman, and F. C. Little as temporary secretary. It was but a short matter to adopt the constitution previously prepared by the preliminary committee and to elect officers. [Steel became first president.] When this was completed all soon began the descent. Before descending, three carrier pigeons were released carrying dispatches; and during several hours signal smokes and mirror flashes were seen in many places in the Willamette valley and in eastern Oregon. It must be considered one of the most remarkable successes in the history of mountaineering that 193 persons (154 men, 39 women) climbed to the summit of this mountain...in one day, and that not one of them suffered an accident of any kind.

"A part of the red fire intended for the summit was burned the same evening on the top of one of the lower moraines and was clearly seen in Portland."

Thus was launched an organization which has flourished to this day, with members in all parts of the globe. Great scientists, educators, men and women famous in public works, leaders in every calling, have been on its rolls. The Mazamas launched studies such as those of our Northwest glaciers, assisting Dr. Harry F. Reid, leading authority of his day on glaciology. From the start they recognized that the Cascades and the Olympic Mountains had been scarcely traveled, Fuller wrote, giving them a special field for work, greater in extent and "more promising in the minds of many of the mountaineers is the annual attainment of special and previously unknown knowledge regarding the glacial peaks and extensive ranges."

This recognition has continued.

13. In a Summit Snow Cave

A novel procession started up Mount Hood four days after the 1894 Mazama organization climb. Two horses, hitched in tandem to a large sled, toiled within a mile of Crater Rock dragging the impedimenta of 10 persons who intended to stay all night. It must have been heavy because after the horses gave out the baggage was sorted into packs and the laden humans sank to their hips in the soft snow.

Finally on top at dusk the weary party went to Mazama Rock and huddled in a gully along one edge, out of the wind. They found two men there comfortably lolling in caverns they had dug in the snow, and the latecomers proceeded to do as they did.

The party made tea over an oil lamp but there was just enough for Ida McElvain, Buckner Wash., the first woman to spend a night on the peak. That night they twice illuminated the summit with red fire and tar smoke, the first time such a display had been made from the very top. They turned in for a fairly comfortable rest, disturbed only by the knowledge they were sleeping one foot from the edge of a 1000-foot drop. They stayed in their blankets until mid-morning, waiting for the sun to soften the ice on the crater wall. As they descended some of the men entered a cavern at the head of White River Glacier where fumaroles were emitting heavy fumes, and registered temperatures of 190 degrees at the vents. On Crater Rock they melted snow in their cups over another vent that registered 170 degrees.

Prince L. Campbell, later president of the University of Oregon, headed the party that made all these firsts on the peak. In addition to Mrs. McElvain the group included C. C. Lewis, Eldon Hale, O. P. Hutchinson, Richard Burford, and two men named Loomis and Ross.

The Mazamas held an outing at Mount Hood in 1901. Their camp on the Francis C. Little homestead was attended by 175 persons. Dr. Harry Fielding Reid, of the Johns Hopkins University, Baltimore, camped there while on a study of the glaciers. At this time a glacier on the west side of Mount Hood, just north of Illumination Rock, was named for him by the Mazamas.

One of the several climbs attempted during this outing made history because of a unique rescue made of a climber who became ill in a storm. Oliver Yocum was in charge of the party, leading a string of 15; a second section of 7 was headed by C. H. Sholes. The weather prospect was not the best but Yocum believed it would improve during the day. Snow conditions were poor and "more trying to the muscles than Guide Yocum had found it in any previous ascent," according to an account in *Mazama* by C. H. Ames, of Boston, a member of the Appalachian Club.

Many of the climbers were near exhaustion when they reached the steeps immediately beneath Crater Rock. The air was cold, skies cloudy, and fog drifted over the summit. On this slope a Portland woman gave out first, and for the 500 feet remaining to Crater Rock, she had to be supported. With much relief the climbers finally gained the rocks.

"By this time," Ames wrote, "the cold was rapidly increasing and a searching wind was arising. The crevices of rock where volcanic heat was evident were sought out, but being exposed to the wind, these were available only for melting ice in tincups and not at all for warming chilled and shivering bodies. Very speedily the whole party found itself huddled closely in a little hollow of rocks on the northern and least exposed side. Here a rude wall seemed to have been thrown up by former visitors. A few more rocks were hastily added."

Hardly had this been done when sleet set in, followed soon by snow. Meanwhile the Sholes party was progressing up the slope to the crater. They shouted for help. The Ames account continues:

"The call...was instantly answered, several members of the first party rushing down over the slope and assisting Sholes and the men to carry Julia Hall, who had become exhausted at the foot of the last steep slope, and Bethel Rawson, who had utterly collapsed and was insensible. The couch of rocks was of the rudest sort, but the two girls were carried there, and attempts made to restore consciousness to Miss Rawson. She remained in complete collapse, despite vigorous chafing of her hands and attempts to administer some drops of brandy and water."

Three men had preceded these two parties to the steep snow above, and heard the shouts for help. Compelled to yield to the tempest they returned to the bivouac at Crater Rock and assisted in the arduous work that followed. Yocum announced that the party would descend as speedily as possible. The exhausted climbers had recovered sufficiently except Miss Rawson. Yocum led the way and, Ames relates, "almost like magic the main body of the party vanished into the snow mist. Five men suddenly found themselves alone in the little nook on Crater Rock, at an altitude of 10,000 feet, in bitter cold, able to see but a few feet in any direction and with the responsibility of the rescue of an unconscious and helpless young woman weighing 120 pounds."

In that group were Sholes, Ames, Professors F. M. McElfresh and F. C. McLouth of Oregon State College, and Henry DeMoss. Cramped in a corner of the rock shelter, Ames for an hour had partially supported the girl. The five men lifted the seemingly lifeless body, staggered over the fringe of rock, and out into the stormy, steep ice slope, "with its thin and treacherous covering of snow, and with the knowledge that a misstep would set us rolling toward a dangerous crevasse at its base below."

"Just how we ever got over the next 200 or 300 yards and down past the end of the crevasse, I doubt if any of us has any very clear notion. It was a period of acutest strain of muscle and mind. We were cumbered more or less with field glasses, knapsacks, etc., and all carried alpenstocks. There were changes of hand grasp as we clutched the helpless girl in whatever way was available for the moment. Sometimes one or two thrust alpenstocks firmly under the ice against which some of the feet of those who carried might be steadied. Sometimes it was four and sometimes all five who helped sustain the living burden.

"Somehow we did find ourselves sinking with our burden in

a demoralized heap at the foot of the first and worst pitch and beyond the worst danger of the crevasse, The dropped hats, field glasses, alpenstocks etc., were assembled as far as possible and we rested for a moment the strained muscles and lungs, but each realizing the hopelessness of extending this experience over any but the smallest portion of the miles between us and camp. Often to each of us came the wretched thought that this prolonged coma might, unless we could speedily change the conditions, be the precursor of death."

So continues the narrative of a New Englander who was getting his first experience in mountaineering in the west. What was the next move? Miss Rawson could not be abandoned there in the storm. If only there was a sled or toboggan — the wish suggested the idea. Professor McElfresh took from his shoulders a thin board frame that he had carried all day in the hope of using it as a toboggan on the descent if the snow was hard enough.

He sat upon the board, took the girl in his arms and told his companions to drag him by the feet. Sholes produced a stout cord. This was looped around McElfresh's ankles and the tow began. It failed instantly as the board sank into the snow. Then came the inspiration credited with saving the girl's life, the idea of a human toboggan, a man's body as the rescue sled.

The cord around his ankles now was passed around the girl's also, and a double line 10 feet long remained for the others to pull the pair. Enough line was left to tie to the man's left arm as a guy rope, which another could hold to keep the human sled from rolling sideways down the slope. The professor now clasped his arms over the girl, as she lay upon him face upward, and signaled for the start. The steep slope was an advantage. Down rushed the singular procession. The "toboggan" plowed a deep groove in the snow but drew more easily than anyone expected.

Suddenly the group emerged from the squall that had clamped its fury close to the summit. Far down the slope the men could see the others who had got a head start from Crater Rock. Eventually some of them were overtaken as the slope grew less and the labor greater. The climbing rope was attached and many hands helped complete the journey to timberline. Only 45 minutes elapsed from Crater Rock to timberline, a distance of 3 miles. For days afterward the groove made by that human toboggan was visible from Government Camp.

At timberline, they found a ready horse and Professor McLouth, with the others supporting the still unconscious girl in front of the saddle, took her to the camp several miles farther down. Five hours after being stricken at Crater Rock, she returned to consciousness under a doctor's care; two days later she was home.

Professor McElfresh claimed he suffered only from being "a little cold and wet." Mountain folk who have experienced the watersoaked slush that often coats the surface of summer snow on a high peak can shiver in sympathy, knowing how completely wet and cold this "human toboggan" got that day.

14. Thirty-One Years of Guiding

Elijah Coalman, the mountain guide around whom center many of the most thrilling stories of human activity on Mount Hood, was born in 1882 in the beautiful Sandy River valley — within sound and sight of the waters that flow from the west side glaciers. He stood on the slopes of the peak while still a tiny youngster. He began getting his "mountain legs" almost as soon as he learned to walk, and for more than 50 years few days passed when Mount Hood was not within his vision.

His mother died when he was very young. His father, Stephen Davis Coalman, who homesteaded east of Sandy in 1862, was one of the incorporators of the Mount Hood and Barlow Toll Road Company, and he worked for many years maintaining the road, taking the boy along on trips across the high passes. They ranged from Gate Creek, near Wamic on the east side, to the west entrance of the toll road at Alder Creek, the son riding in front of his father's saddle. As a youth he too worked on the road.

O. C. Yocum, Lije Coalman's predecessor as guide, homesteaded at Government Camp. Father and son sometimes stopped at the Yocum resort. Yocum took Coalman on his first climb in August 1897 when he was 15 years old. While working on the road, Lije often assisted Yocum in escorting parties to the summit, and he made five ascents in the first year. He climbed again in 1898, 1901, and every season thereafter until 1928. During Portland's 1905 Lewis and Clark Exposition, when Government Camp had many visitors, Coalman guided his own party for the first time.

After Yocum retired in 1908, Coalman had 47 climbing parties in 1909 and about the same number the next year, after which he began building Government Camp Hotel. As the first Yocum establishment was built in 1900, this building was known as the annex. (Both were swept away in the noonday fire of October 1933.) In 1910 Coalman took over the Yocum homestead of 160 acres, and that autumn started work on the hotel. It was a tall building, though of only three stories, with a steep-pitched roof to bear the weight of winter snows. It was designed for 50 guests and was placed in operation before it was finished in 1912.

From the onset, inadequate roads to Government Camp made the large hotel an uncertain financial venture. Coalman sold his hotel and 40 acres in 1914 to Dell Fox and L. F. Pridemore. The other 120 acres went to D. C. Latourette of Oregon City, who later acquired the hotel and the rest of the land. The following year saw Coalman guiding and also establishing a lookout on the summit, and he remained a Forest Service employe on the high station for four seasons. The rough life and serious injuries he suffered in connection with his work on the mountain top told heavily. He climbed only occasionally between 1919 and 1923. In 1924 he returned as a guide in the employ of J. V. Rafferty, who had taken over the hotel. That was his last year in such work, although he continued leading parties whose members sought him out. But the strain on his body became too great and in 1928 he made his last ascent — his 586th.

Thus, a brief chronology of Elijah Coalman's association with Mount Hood. He gave safe escort to many hundreds of climbers. On top as lookout he kept vigilant eye not only over the forests for fires but for the climbers, and when he saw signs of distress, went to their assistance.

Unless one is "hardened in" for the effort, the climb is exhausting. It was much worse when parties had to start from Government Camp, ascending first through the forest, then over the snowfields, a full 8 miles to the top. Always there have been persons attempting the ascent with inadequate clothing and equipment, booted poorly and carrying improper food or eating snow, nauseated by the gases in the crater, frightened by the sheer heights, weakened by too strenuous work in the rare air of 10,000 feet and above. The summit has been the scene often of the most poignant human distress. Of all the types of misery a man encounters, the woe of a tired, sickened mountain climber is in a class alone. Here is an ill he cannot go to bed with. He is beset when almost at his goal. He has the choice of grinding on or turning back. Pride demands that he finish the job.

Hordes of wretches like these have poked their weary heads above the rim to see Coalman's huge, freckled hand reaching out to help. In the warmth of his cabin on top they have had tea and hot soup and, with returning strength, climbed the ladder into his tower to look over the country he knew so well.

In the summer of 1916 a party of eight ascended the peak by the Cooper's Spur route. They reached the summit at 11 AM, and because of other engagements were forced to start the descent in a few minutes. In one of the steep rocky gullies below the summit a slide started. The others were able to dodge the flying bits but a girl was struck in the temple and fell unconscious. From on top, Coalman had been watching the party because he feared the leader did not know the mountain sufficiently, so he hurried down and carried the girl back to the summit.

George Miller, a north side guide, assisted in the attempt to restore her but he and Coalman decided she needed a doctor's care for her injury. They broke up a table in the cabin to obtain a board, wrapped the semi-conscious girl in blankets and lashed her to it. She was carried down the south side, the litter sliding in the chute where possible, and lowered into and across three crevasses because the ladders bridging them were too flimsy to carry the weight of three adults. Meanwhile a rescue party, summoned by telephone, met the group on the snowfields.

Two weeks later a party of Mountaineers from Seattle ascended the north side. Below the great brow at the top, where climbers are out of sight from the summit, they did not reappear as expected, so Coalman went to the west edge of the summit ridge from where he could see down under the steep. He spied the party gathered closely at the head of Cooper's Spur, and it was plain they were in trouble. He hurried down and found a woman had been struck by a rock and a deep wound inflicted in one hip. He applied a compress and bandaged the cut, then slid with her as far as possible. George Miller, who had been summoned from Cloud Cap by phone, met them and took the woman by toboggan, thence on horseback to the Inn.

When Coalman was guiding again in 1924 and George Phelps was the lookout, a couple from Iowa attempted the south side climb alone. They were in the chute and crossing an avalanche groove, scoured out by fragments falling from the cliffs; the guides avoid these dangerous places. Five hundred feet from the top a falling rock fractured the man's thigh. His wife climbed up and summoned Phelps who, after notifying the ranger station below, went down and made the man as comfortable as possible on a shelf leveled in the ice.

George Calverly, a packer, and Coalman went up with horses, traversing the snowfield west of Triangle Moraine. Calverly started to ride around what he thought was the end of a crevasse when his horse slipped on a thin bridge over a "blind" ice crack. He barely had time to save himself when the horse plunged through, dropping out of sight 30 feet under a lip. Nothing could be done to save the animal, nor to go down and put an end to its sufferings — the only rope long enough was on the saddle.

Coalman left his own horse on the moraine and went on with Calverly to the injured man. Phelps joined in carrying him back to the horse, and he was taken to the settlement. Calverly later returned with rope and recovered his saddle and other equipment from the dead horse.

In 1916 a search was being conducted around Zig Zag and Sand canyons for a young Portlander who was lost for two nights and a day. Coalman, who from his station on top had been searching with field glasses, saw the youth walking on a snowfield near Mississippi Head. Coalman made a descent by a slide of unsurpassed daring. Taking off down the chute, he steered west of the hogsback and, going at a tremendous clip, slid through the precipitous narrow runway at the head of Zig Zag Glacier, a trough so steep that climbers shun it. He glissaded a third of the way, then ran in the amazing lope with which he often descended the mountain, sliding again where he found slopes steep enough. He reached the youth in 11 minutes!

There are hosts of stories such as this.

In the summer of 1912 while he was completing the Government Camp Hotel, Coalman saw a party on their way, then finished some other chores before starting out to guide them to the top. He was anxious about the lifeline cable in the chute and decided to look it over before his string of patrons took to its support. From timberline to the top Coalman made the ascent in 98 minutes, a distance covered by the average party in 6 to 8 hours or longer. After overhauling the line he descended, met the group below Crater Rock and turned back upwards with them.

Dee Wright, forest service packer, and Coalman were close friends. In the summer of 1917 while working with a string of pack animals west of Government Camp, Dee was kicked in the chest by Dynamite, a mule that had often carried loads to Crater Rock. He asked that word be sent to Coalman, who was on the summit.

By sliding and running, Coalman reached timberline in 13 minutes; 11 minutes later he was at Dee's bedside. The injury suffered was, a few years later, a contributing cause of Wright's death. By coincidence a similar injury that year was to exact complications that made it necessary for Coalman to stop living at lofty elevations.

While the Fuhrer brothers were south side guides, Hans suffered a serious injury when he fell on his ice ax while glissading from the hogsback down into the crater. Coalman, who was on top, said he had cautioned the Swiss mountaineer against glissading without covering the head of his ax, but Hans replied that Europeans did without this precaution. He saw Hans's group at Crater Rock, greatly agitated, while one member hurried down the mountain and others tried to attract Coalman's attention. He took his first aid bag and slid, not down the chute, but farther east, where the slope is steeper and avalanches stream to the bottom. From the top of the hogsback he slid again into the crater and ran across to the Rock.

The ice ax had ripped open Fuhrer's abdomen. Coalman bandaged and splinted the wound tightly, even sewing the dressings, then picked up the Swiss — almost as heavy as himself — and slid with and carried him to timberline, to a waiting horse.

The cabin at timberline, near the head of Sand Canyon, used as a rest stop on the climb and a refuge for skiers, was known to everyone as Camp Blossom. Coalman insisted this was wrong, that Camp Blossom, so named by Oliver Yocum, was the area at the upper end of the old road from Government Camp, long abandoned. The late Judge M. C. George, past leader of the Mazamas, was fond of camping with his family at Blossom. The camp became so large that the judge found his old site crowded, so he moved west to the meadows in which the building stands. Coalman said the place henceforth was known as Camp George and the building should have been so named.

Events overtook the popular old site, which was widely assumed to be the future location of Timberline Lodge. But when the Forest Service made the decision, it was shifted several hundred yards eastward. That site has the advantage of a fine glade giving a good view of the peak above, and it is close to both the Eastleg and Westleg roads.

Many of the fires that Coalman saw from the summit were north of the mountain, and because of the delay in passing the reports by telephone around from the south side, a line was strung to Cloud Cap Inn. On the higher stretches it was necessary to lay these wires in the snow and because of avalanches, weather breaks and other mishaps, the line required much maintaining.

In August 1917 Coalman was returning to the top from a repair job at Cooper's Spur when an avalanche of rock came down. He tried to dodge but a boulder struck him squarely in the chest and knocked him unconscious. He rolled down the slope into a trough at one end of the Crescent crevasse where he lay for almost an hour. When he came to, his whole body felt numb. In his shirt pocket, the metal case of his sunglasses was smashed and a packet of letters were torn by the blow. But doctors told him this padding had saved him from mortal injury.

Coalman knew he was injured badly, and his first thought was to get back to Government Camp via the east side across Newton Clark Glacier. That effort seemed too great so he went down the Spur to the Inn, which was empty, and he spent a night in agony. The following day, breathless from pain, he crawled back up to the lookout station, and there was able barely to telephone for help. He stayed overnight, then descended to Crater

Rock where a horse was brought, and soon was taken to Portland for treatment.

Mark Weygandt, who had guided for many years on the north side, took Coalman's place as lookout for the rest of the season. Coalman returned in 1918 but he was "washed up;" the blow damaged his heart and made his last summer on the rim one of misery. George Maroney, who did the packing from Crater Rock and kept up the phone lines, was assigned as helper.

The 1919 season saw another man keeping the mountain top vigil and to those who knew it in Lije's day, the summit establishment never again seemed quite as attractive.

15. A Strike at Ten Thousand Feet

On the many trips he made to the summit, Elijah Coalman often reported forest fires. In 1914 Bruce Osborne invented the fire locating instrument that revolutionized the system of forest fire detection and suppression; he made the climb with Coalman, who suggested the possibility of a lookout station on top of Mount Hood. Coalman wrote a letter to Forest Supervisor Tom Sherrard asking that one of the new finders be mounted on top, with a telephone link and a tent for the lookout's home.

Once his plan was approved, Coalman's first task was the telephone line, and he completed the hookup from timberline in three days. Dee Wright, the packer, carried a roll of insulated emergency cable on a horse to Turtleneck, at the head of the moraine west of White River Glacier. George Ledford, the ranger at Summit Meadows, and Coalman strung the wire.

A tent was designed to meet the strenuous requirements of a mountain-top abode. It tapered to a cone-like peak, but 12 feet square at the base. The heaviest available canvas was used — doubled, a tent within a tent — with seams and ties reinforced with leather. To support it Coalman brought a cedar post, six inches thick and 14 feet long, with iron fittings at the top for steel cables to guy the tent to the rocks. This was an excellent precaution in a place where winds of hurricane force blew frequently. The tent was set up just 14 feet from the towering wall above Eliot Glacier.

Wright transported other equipment to a cache near the base of Crater Rock. Coalman, Ledford and Osborne then back-packed it in 80- to 100-pound loads the rest of the way, and the lookout occupied this novel habitation the first time on July 10 1915.

The tent was floored. Cooking was done and the place heated with kerosene stoves, which Coalman lugged up from the cache. With little assistance Coalman continued this back-packing between elevations of 9,000 and 11,235 feet for four seasons.

Soon an electric storm occurred and the lightning spotted the forest with fires. Coalman located them quickly and the utility of the high reporting station was proved. Not long after taking his post Coalman turned in a "smoke," far north at the edge of the snowfields on the south side of Mount Adams. The alarm was relayed to the Columbia National Forest in Washington, and a fireman hurried to the scene. It was a fire, sure enough, but one started by Coalman's friends, the Mazamas, who were cleaning up camp at Cold Spring after a Mount Adams climb. Between July 10 and August 25 Coalman reported 131 fires.

Life in the tent was rough. The tall lookout had to spend most of his time on hands and knees. He was bothered by fumes from the stove. A tiring trip to the cache, usually made very early in the morning or after dark so as to lose no time from fire observation, was a daily chore. Osborne continued his interest and long before the season was over he began talking up the building of a cabin.

Late in August the Forest Service asked Coalman for suggestions on a cabin design. His plan was accepted, the building ordered, and he made an excavation 3 feet deep and 12 feet square, on the highest point a few feet south of the parapet of Eliot wall. When lumber was delivered at Government Camp, Coalman cut and prepared it for transport to the summit.

The materials were sorted into bundles weighing 60 to 80 pounds, so they could be handled by both horses and men without being reassembled. Wright gathered 14 pack animals, most of them the biggest mules he could find, for the lift to Crater Rock. Total weight of the cabin was about 8000 pounds, but the task was completed in eight days. Ranger Ledford recruited a crew of the huskiest men available, and their camp was set up near the cache.

Coalman returned to the summit September 6 with Roy Mitchell as chief assistant. The packers gathered at Crater Rock about the same time and began work. Then came the strike.

The loads went up steadily the first day but the night was cold, the camp uncomfortable and, next morning, there was much complaining as the packers arrived. Even the strongest found it exhausting labor, and Coalman was not surprised when word came that the packers felt their pay of 1-1/2 cents a pound — i.e., 90 cents for a 60 pound load! — was too low. They wanted 2 cents. He telephoned Ranger Ledford who rode up on a horse. A violent argument ensued at Crater Rock. It ended when Coalman agreed to the 2 cents demand, and Sherrard backed him.

Four of the men had enough, however, and left the mountain. Of the 10 continuing, 4 quit before another day, then 3 more gave up. The crew was now only 6, Hans and Heinie Fuhrer, George Maroney, Marshall Davis, Mitchell and Coalman. They took a week to finish the job. Coalman carried the last load — a keg of nails, hinges and hardware, altogether 120 pounds.

The climbing route at that time was east of the way followed in 1937. [*Because of change by erosion, this is the route regularly used today.*] It ascended the hogsback, then rose directly up the steep snowfield for 1000 feet reaching to the top of the summit ridge. Where the base of this snowfield and the hogsback join (the place that mountaineers call "the break") a crevasse opens about mid-season and by September it usually is a deep yawning fissure. So it was in 1915. In places it was 80 feet from lip to bottom, and rocks from the cliffs hurtled into it. The packer had to face this rugged pile far below as he crawled gingerly over the ladder-bridge across the chasm.

No one who crossed that ladder could forget the experience. Coalman made it from scraps — a flimsy thing 18 feet long, with steps far apart because lumber was scarce. It creaked and swayed and groaned and rolled because its ends barely reached the walls of ice at each end, and the top rung had been hooked over a knob of frozen snow. For greater security the anchored lifeline, strung down from the summit, was tied to the top of the ladder.

Small wonder the packers demanded a one-third pay increase after traversing the rickety ladder a few times with their heavy loads. Coalman himself, a big man, confessed to being frightened when he crossed it. Worse still, the surface snow had melted, leaving the permanent ice exposed — a hummocky surface with cuplike depressions. It was a dirty greenish gray, as desolate a sight as Mount Hood ever presents. The crevasse, Coalman declared, was the largest he had ever seen at that point. It extended across the entire slope.

On top, a framework of 2 by 8 timbers laminated to make 10 by 10's was laid in the bottom of the excavation and heavily braced. Coalman began building up from that, and when all construction was above the surface he filled the excavation with rocks. He laid a double floor and bridged the framework for greater strength. The center post, reaching up into the observation cupola, was another laminated 10 by 10 but these long members had to be pieced out since the greatest length he had was only 8 feet. The walls were four layers thick, two outside the framing and two inside, with building paper between each layer.

Coalman and Mitchell, working against time, were beset by a tempest which nearly cost them their lives. The blast hit with such force they had to crawl 100 yards to their tent. The gale drove a sleety rain, horizontally, freezing as it struck. Before morning they were prisoners in a castle of ice, and for three days and two nights they remained there, watching their canvas walls come closer and closer as the heavy frozen mass increased. They were not able to stand or even kneel, but managed, while lying in their sleeping bags, to heat some food. Beds, stove, men and supplies were all jammed into a space less than half of what it had been. The sturdy cedar pole supporting the peak bent almost double and the desperate men beneath were forced to prop it. Continually, too, they were haunted by the unnerving thought of that precipice above Eliot Glacier a few feet away. They could not see out — for all they knew the guy wires might have snapped and they were at the edge.

As quickly as possible when the storm abated they cut a hole through the ice — now 30 inches thick. On the stormy side, the ice had built up in a great 4-ft. mound against the canvas. Because they could not get to their telephone outside the tent, no one below knew of their plight. Rescue in any event would have been impossible as the mountain could not be climbed.

At the end of September Coalman and Mitchell had completed the work except for the cupola. Another storm was brewing and they did not care to repeat their experience. Food and fuel were about exhausted anyway, so they retreated to the lowlands. On that day the storm set in. While Coalman remained to make fast, Mitchell started down to remove the long lifeline; in the frozen snow, after loosening the line at top, he began to cut steps. The handle of his ice ax broke and he returned to fit a new one. As dusk was settling the two started down again, Coalman carrying his personal belongings in a 70-pound pack and steadying himself with an alpenstock. Mitchell was ahead cutting steps when his ice ax broke again.

He then took the alpenstock to gouge out footings, leaving Coalman to depend on his nailed boots to prevent slipping. It was dark before they had gone halfway to the crevasse. The line was gone. It was snowing and the force of the wind was so great they could scarcely stand. Crawling along, they reached the brink of the crevasse. A rope had been left at the ladder anchorage, looped around the ice buttress at the top.

In the black storm cloud they reached the crevasse too far west and had to edge along the steep lip hunting for the ladder. While doing this Coalman, having no way to steady himself, was caught off balance by a gust of wind and in an instant was hurtling, in a sitting position, toward the brink. With presence of mind he remembered that the lower face of the crevasse sloped while the upper was vertical, and a shelf was midway down on the lower side. As he went over the edge he shoved hard with his hands and slammed against the lower wall instead of making a sheer drop. He hit the shelf, then slid 35 feet to the bottom. Snow on the rocks cushioned his fall but he sprained both ankles and one knee.

From his pack he tore a towel into strips and tightly bandaged his injured joints. Meanwhile Mitchell crept along to the ladder anchorage. The rope was gone; it had been looped loosely and the wind whipped it into the crevasse. Coalman was able to make his way at the bottom and recover the rope, then climb to where he could throw it up to Mitchell — in a dozen tries. Mitchell then descended to the crevasse shelf where he could help Coalman climb out over the lower side.

Although painfully crippled, Coalman struggled on down. In the storm the pair drifted eastward. At timberline they had to cross toward the west to find the Government Camp trail. By chance Coalman, swinging the alpenstock, struck the telephone wire, and so regained their bearings. At 2 am they reached the Government Camp Hotel, where Coalman was laid up for three weeks.

The lookout cabin withstood such great storms for 22 years. Forest Service records show its total cost was $632.92.

Although semi-disabled, Coalman worked at a variety of jobs at Portland and Sandy, then at Spirit Lake, Mount St. Helens, finally in retirement in California for 30 years. He died June 29 1970 at Santa Rosa. His ashes were scattered on Mount Hood.

16. Measuring Its Heights

"How high is Mount Hood?"

This question is asked most frequently about the physical features of the peak, and strange to say, there remains doubt about the exact altitude. The 1937 figure given on government maps is 11,253 feet but in some quarters this is questioned. Lewis A. McArthur, whose business over many years has brought him in touch with land measurement problems, has studied Oregon history, place names and elevations as a hobby. He is consulted by many agencies in these matters and his opinion that the elevation given is too high has much weight.

For 50 years the mountain's height was held to be 11,225 feet. It was calculated in 1867 by Lieutenant Colonel R. S. Williamson, an army engineer, and was accepted as standard. When the Mount Hood quadrangle was mapped in 1907–1911 by the U. S. Geological Survey, the mark was checked and held correct. A later check by the U. S. Coast and Geodetic Survey, however, computed the higher figure, but McArthur claims that the bench marks or known base elevations have since proved to be off — that they are listed higher than the true elevation and, in consequence, any determinations made from these bases would be above their real heights. C&GS publications gave two elevations for the mountain, one 11,224 and the other 11,253. Both were determined by precise triangulation, the figures being obtained from vertical angle measurement, some of which were shot at considerable distance from the peak. McArthur believed the plane table work by the Geological Survey was more nearly correct.

McNeil writes official figures for 1937. Further studies and calculations have changed it again and again. In August 1958 Pilot Bill Hartley landed a Bell helicopter on the mountain top — quite a feat for that aircraft. USGS Geologist Conrad Merrick remembers the wind was dead calm on top that day, so Hartley could not carry a geologist along. He was assigned to set up reflectors, with which the USGS men made precise measurements.

Glenn W. Ireland, a cartographer of the Portland USGS office, expects the official height to change in future, with ever more precise methods. Based on 1988 data the agency places Mount Hood's summit at 11,239 feet above sea level.

Aside from human error, which we cannot avoid, no figure given for Mount Hood's top could be called permanent, because the mountain is changing constantly, growing and receding all at once. Erosion never ceases; large masses slide continuously from the walls of the crater. Ice is tearing it to pieces. The summit ridge is thin, and those long acquainted with the peak see it altered. Photographs show that the slope off the uppermost part of the crest becomes more abrupt. There is not nearly so much area as was the case in 1910. Likewise, the saddle west of the highest point has become deeper and more acute. The mountain is slowly falling away and, quite likely, an accurate measurement now would show a lower figure than any yet given.

There was much speculation in early days over the height of the peak. It was generally accepted that the tip was 14,000 to 17,000 feet above the sea. A note of pride runs through an assertion published about 1868 that Oregon had a peak "superior in height to the great mounts of the Andes, in the southern Cordillera." Challenges to such hyperbole by serious scientists were criticized by editors determined to cling to the larger figures, and it must have been a great blow for them to accept Colonel Williamson's report. He made his computation with carefully adjusted barometers, a method that would not be used in precise measurements now. Nevertheless he came very close.

Williamson finished his task August 23 1867 with stations for barometric comparison at Astoria, Fort Vancouver and The Dalles, and, for a few days previous to the ascent, at Government Camp and timberline on Mount Hood. He was accompanied by Lieutenant W. H. Heuer, John T. Best, observer, and eight soldiers. Thermal barometers, cistern barometers and wet and dry bulb thermometers were among the equipment carried up the mountain. Only three of the soldiers reached the top with the leaders. Most of the afternoon was spent in adjusting the instruments and recording. Elaborate computations were necessary but, essentially, the determination was made by comparison of the findings at the various stations from sea level to the top.

The reading at timberline gave an elevation of 5952 feet. The elevation of Camp Blossom is just above the 6000-ft. mark. At Government Camp Meadow an elevation of 3864 feet was reported. With the modesty of the true scientist, Colonel Williamson said of his findings, "I think they will not differ 100 feet from the estimates here given," when he recommended further studies.

Three years later, Professor G. H. Collier, of Pacific University, and eight students joined Professor L. J. Powell, of Salem, and climbed with a barometer which was given careful attention on the summit. After an afternoon of observations, the altitude was announced as 11,218 feet.

Mount Hood stands on the crest of the Cascade range, 25 miles south of the Columbia River; 50 miles and a little south of east from Portland. It is the highest point in Oregon; timber grows to an elevation of 6500 feet. Of the great snow sentinels of the Pacific Northwest, it is third in rank, Rainier and Adams surpassing in elevation. Its rise above the common general elevation is about 6000 feet.

Carl Price Richards was the Mazama club's No. 1 realist. He was an engineer and, before his trained mind, cherished illusions about Mount Hood have fell, one by one. Some of these date back to the earliest climbers and nurtured along, generation through generation, they were given wide credibility.

Chief of these, perhaps, was the impression that Mount Shasta, in northern California, could be seen from the top of Mount Hood. There were many who doubted, among them Richards. His questing mind asked, is it possible to see this peak, 275.1 miles away?

His reply appears in the Mazama annuals of 1927 and '28, and while it is complex reading, the essence is that Shasta is out of view. Its elevation is 14,380 feet, and considering Hood's top at 11,253, a few feet either way makes no difference; the problem was whether each was visible from the other above the earth's curvature. From the top of Mount Hood the distance to the apparent south horizon was shown to be 105.4 miles, while the observer on Mount Shasta would see the horizon 129.3 miles north. These total 234.7 miles — 40.4 miles short of the 275.1 miles between the two mountains. The line of vision from one to the other would be obscured by the surface.

This calculation was based on the assumption that the country lying between, the very backbone of the Cascades, is 5000 feet above sea level. In fact, it is higher, and numerous high peaks intervene to further obstruct the view.

At the time the call was made for interested people to climb Mount Hood to organize the Mazamas in 1894, it was said that among the many attractions would be the sight of the Pacific to the west. Explanations were saved that day, if questions had come up, by the fact that clouds obscured the horizon. Since then many have claimed to have seen the ocean and have written beautiful accounts of the sun setting in the sea.

This also came under Richards's fire. He showed that a line from the summit to the nearest point on the coast, Netarts, is 109 miles. Using similar methods as before, he figured the sea level horizon from the top of Mount Hood at 139.86 miles. Thus, claims of seeing the ocean would appear to be good, with perhaps 30 miles to spare. The intervening factor is the Coast range, whose crest is 82 miles west at a height of about 2000 feet. Coast range passes, some of them under 1000 feet, are masked by interlacing hills on both sides. The line of vision to the sea horizon was shown to pass the 82-mile point at 1910 feet, which is under the skyline of the Coast range. Beyond the range summit are many other hills of similar height, and with the sea-level line declining on a constant, Richards holds that it would be lost among them. A small hill at the coast would obstruct the view as much as the summit of the range - much higher, farther inland. The inevitable conclusion, he declares, is that you cannot see the ocean from our peak. For the same reason Mount Hood cannot be seen from vessels in the Pacific.

To the problem of relative sizes of the "Guardians of the Columbia" Richard applied himself. He used methods easy for an engineer but too complex for this book. He found that, considering Mount Adams as the unit, Mount Hood's volume relationship is 0.375, Mount St. Helens's 0.106 — 0.473 added together, or less than half the bulk of Mount Adams. When measured above the 5000-foot level, the size of that mountain, however, is only 27.45 cubic miles, compared to 48.95 cubic miles for Mount Rainier. Mount Hood, measured this way, is estimated at 10.07 cubic miles.

Mid-section measurement of Mount Hood, west to east, shows a diameter of about 7 miles at the 5000-foot level, and from north to south, 8 miles. The latter is the expanse of the mountain that is seen from Portland, as most of the base below 5000 feet is obscured by subsidiary folds.

17. The Glacial Tiara

The slopes of Mount Hood support 10 identifiable glaciers, seven of them well defined: one masked and somewhat indefinite as to boundary and area; an "inter-glacier" that, due to isolated position, has received sparse attention; and a small remnant of slightly active ice stream, on the north side.

A popular trip with the more arduous-minded mountaineers is to make the circuit of these icefields high up on the peak. Such a hike we may picture here for a quick survey. We start from *Eliot* because it is the most accessible due to the road's end a short distance away at Cloud Cap Inn. With slight effort one can step on its frozen field. Eliot Glacier is the largest and the most characteristic. The great ice mass on the northeast flank of the peak has had more study than any other. Avalanches, thundering down the wall back of the cirque that reaches to the summit, have awed throngs of visitors at Cloud Cap.

Our circuit of the mountain will be counter-clockwise. After crossing Eliot, and ascending it a ways too, we step on *Coe* Glacier, which heads far up the northwest ridge, in a grand flourish almost to timberline. The *neve* reservoir of Coe also feeds Ladd Glacier, next one to the left, and these two ice streams mingle in the great portal between the upper end of Barrett Spur and Pulpit Rock.

Beyond Ladd, separated from it by two high ridges and with its long narrow lobe occupying a canyon all its own, is the inter-glacier, a completely independent stream that is drained by one branch of Ladd Creek. To many it is known as Eden Park Glacier, but the name does not appear on maps. The drainage to this point has been into the forks of the Hood River.

Across Cathedral Ridge we enter the Sandy Watershed, which takes all the water off the west and south sides of the mountain. Beyond the broad *Sandy* Glacier we cross Yocum Ridge and come upon a magnificent spectacle, the rugged, cascading *Reid* Glacier, which seems to leap from terrace to terrace down a deep gorge from Illumination Rock. One will go far to see a glacier more precipitously pitched. It is filled with towering seracs in minareted shapes, pagodas and mushroom heads that lean dangerously as one passes beneath them. The explorer climbing on Reid through these seracs is in canyons of ice whose walls are banded with stratas of luminous hue. Ice caverns are there to be entered, and inside, when the sun shines brightly, the rays give the thinner walls a greenish cast like ocean breakers; deeper, the ice is a blue more striking than the color of Crater Lake.

A gigantic ice fall, where the glacier breaks over a cliff, is seen about halfway up, and one has to climb past it to get to the head, whence we emerge near Illumination Rock. Reid has hewn on the south a wall hundreds of feet high and (most of it) vertical. There are only a few places where this wall may be passed. From Portland it is a black line running westward down the mountain.

At Illumination Rock we are ready to swing eastward, at about 9000 feet elevation, across *Zig Zag* Glacier. The lower half of this one is a broad sheet with few glacial characteristics, but it narrows in a sharp triangle in the upper levels, and where it passes the west side of Crater Rock it is compressed into a narrow ribbon of ice hung at an abrupt angle. In this chute, rock avalanches from both Crater Rock and Hawkins cliff whiz down at tremendous speed.

Zig Zag is one of the two glaciers that have, or once had, their sources in the crater. Between Crater Rock and the summit wall extends the sharp snow wedge commonly known to climbers as the "hogsback." This is thrown up by the action of air currents ascending through the Zig Zag trough. The snow accumulating west of the hogsback, both by precipitation and in dropping from the heights, is the neve of Zig Zag. On the east side of the snow crest is the greater part of the old crater, and the snows there, feed *White River* Glacier. In recent years White River Glacier has been severed at the point where it breaks down the mountain side from the crater, apparently due to the heat of fumaroles. Most of its supply derives from snow that slides off Steel's Cliff and the extension of that ridge down the east side of this glacier. Some observers believe the present sharp recession of White River Glacier is due to this severance at the top.

As we continue over the southern face of the mountain we encounter a large snowfield, rarely recognizable as a glacier. Nevertheless one is there. It takes a hot, dry season, with a preceding winter of little snow, to expose it. *Palmer* Glacier was discovered, explored and classified by Mazamas in 1924. Probably, with Zig Zag it was the first glacier on the mountain to be trod by white men. Joel Palmer went that way in 1845 from Paradise Park when he climbed the southern slopes to look for a route for Barlow's wagon train.

Crossing Palmer and the moraine east of it, we leave the watershed of the Sandy. Palmer's terminal feeds two forks of the Salmon River, the most easterly drainage of the Sandy basin.

White River Glacier waters flow in a turbid torrent into the Deschutes. This glacier is compressed tight in its canyon, and has been known to "boil out" across the comparatively low western moraine and contribute to the Palmer reservoir. White River courses southeast from the rim of the crater. It gets the direct rays of the sun at all seasons, and, being pinched for space its history, as written in the canyon walls and the valley, shows greater change than any of the others. Erosion, it follows, because of the solar influence, is greater here than on other sides of the mountain.

Crossing this glacier we scramble up and over the long ridge below Steel's cliff and traverse *Newton Clark* Glacier, a broad expanse of ice entirely spanning the east side of the mountain. Newton Clark discharges its stream in cascades over lava benches, and frequently avalanches at the cliff below the terminal.

At the northern margin we are at Cooper's Spur and, ascending this great moraine, find ourselves looking again over Eliot — our circuit completed.

Mount Hood's glaciers have been studied for more than a

century. Arnold Hague was the first scientist of note to visit them. Sent out to explore the western mountains by the American Geographic Society, he gave a description of White River Glacier as he saw it in 1871. He said it headed from the east side of the crater, and, at the point where it started breaking down from the mountainside, a broad transverse crevasse cut entirely across the icefield. It is notable here that this investigator said the glacier headed within the crater. In 1882 a steaming fumarole was reported in the glacier at this point.

Where Hague's crevasse then extended, there is now a broad island of lava rubble, bare except in seasonal snows. It was here that the Forest Service in 1934 completed the Crater Rock stone shelter for climbers. That building had scarcely been built before its walls began cracking, and it is now in ruins. A theory for this destruction is that the lava material exists as a surface moraine, with the ancient ice of the White River stream still moving deep beneath it.

By 1907 when A. H. Sylvester studied the mountain, the crack at the head of White River had so expanded that he found the glacier's bed exposed for 150 feet. Sylvester still said the glacier extended back to the northern wall, but just east of Crater Rock there was an immense ice cave caused by a fumarole. Since then several fumaroles have appeared on this isthmus across the glacial bottleneck.

Dr. Harry Reid, Johns Hopkins University geologist, explored the glaciers in 1901. He also said the White River reservoir was in the crater bed. His article in the 1905 *Mazama* is one of the best ever published about these glaciers. After describing the crater, he observed that one would expect the caldera to be the reservoir for all the principal glaciers but such is not the case. Because the crater is small and exposed to intense sunlight, the snow accumulation is not large. For the most part the glacier reservoirs lie farther down the mountain flanks.

With the exception of Reid, the glaciers do not occupy deep depressions but shallow basins, or stand up, supported by their moraines. In the canyon of White River, below the snout, Dr. Reid described a long table-shaped elevation which has come to be called Moraine Mesa, a prominent feature of the mountain. The retreat of the glacier, he said, had been very recent, and Moraine Mesa was ice-covered less than 100 years before 1901.

On the west side there were two glaciers, Reid reported, "one having no name," on Douglas Langille's map of the northern Cascade Forest Reserve. At that time the glacier did have a name — his own, conferred by the Mazamas that same year. In his explorations he made red marks on rocks where his pictures were taken, and these identified spots were used later for comparison by Mazama investigators.

The Mazama research committee, in 1935, guided by Dr. Reid's photos, concluded that White River had receded approximately 1000 feet in 34 years. In 1871 Hague reported that the terminus was 500 feet below timberline. The total recession in 63 years, the Mazamas concluded, was in excess of 4000 feet, with the rate in the latter half of the period apparently lessened.

Reid's photos also show recession of Newton Clark Glacier, compared with conditions today, but at much slower rate than its neighbor just south. In 1901 the ice reached over the edge of a cliff at its main terminus, the frozen wall extending directly above the rock. Today the ice sheet is much thinner and the terminus, 500 feet back of the cliff. (Recession is defined as retreat of a glacier up the mountainside.)

Observations of Eliot Glacier have been extensive. From 1890 to 1896 Will Langille, the Cloud Cap guide, measured the surface flow systematically and found its velocity, in the middle near the lower end, averaged 50 feet a year.

Eliot has been measured by Mazamas nearly every year since 1925. Baselines were set with transits at three points across the field that season. In general, greatest motion was found in the center, the sides being retarded by friction against the moraines. Climatic conditions are responsible chiefly for the changes. Seasons of heavy snowfall retard depletion of the stream the summer following, as the surface snows shield the deposits below from heat, and prevent the opening of crevasses which let warm air into the glacier interior.

The 1926 season was hot and dry, and 15 feet of the Eliot surfaced melted away, it was estimated, while the terminus retreated 15 feet. By 1929 more extensive findings were possible on the basis of the earlier work. In four years the highest line in places had moved 689 feet, the middle one 282 feet, and the advance of the line at 6500 feet elevation was only 37.3 feet. Markers disappeared each season. Out of a dozen placed at 7800 feet in 1925, only two were left in '29. The rest had dropped into crevasses or were buried in the ice. In a year those two had moved 157 and 150 feet, respectively, a rate of about 3 feet a week; movement was faster there because of the steeper slope. At the middle line the glacier had crept forward 1-1/4 feet each week and at the lower one, only 1-1/4 inches.

Recession of Eliot apparently has not been rapid. After a dry summer in 1935 its snout receded 12 feet between September 15 and October 19, but slight advances were shown in 1932–33. One of Dr. Reid's 1901 photos, compared in 1935, showed recession of 240 feet. However, the committee found the ice sheet much thinner at the terminus after that 34-year interval.

At best, a study of this sort is general and admittedly of low accuracy. Many difficulties are encountered with the rough topography, while the terminals are so masked by morainal deposits as to make examination highly speculative. The problem of vertical depletion (thickness of glacial ice) has been barely touched. It has long been known, of course, that live glaciers move, at bottom dissipating into drainage streams while the upper portions are replenished by snow reservoirs and seasonal precipitation. Of great importance to future generations is whether the permanent glacial ice is being depleted so that one day their basins will be bare. How vital this question is can be gauged by knowing that practically all the water irrigating the huge fruit industry of the Hood River valley comes from the glaciers of the snowcap.

Coe Glacier has been measured from a baseline at its terminus which was surveyed in August 1928. Recession was shown every year except 1935, when it advanced, although the same season showed Eliot's snout receding.

In 1927 Ladd was baselined, but measurement has been impeded by surface snow and heavy morainal cover. However, the glacier seems to be in a state of equilibrium. Sandy, Reid and Zig Zag have not been measured but comparison photos show decided recession. In particular, investigators claim Reid has been melting excessively in recent years without compensatory feeding at the top.

In the opinion of Dr. Reid and others, within historic time Mount Hood's glaciers have never been much larger than they are at present. This is indicated by their moraines, which end a short distance beyond the present termini. Large old trees growing just below and in line with the snouts also are held as proof that the glaciers have not been much more extensive in recent centuries.

Discovery of Palmer Glacier was a remarkable event. There have been other years when snow almost vanished from the south side of Mount Hood but in 1924 the meteorological sequence was just right for it. Always before it had been known as a part of the "big snowfield." The open winter and the warm, dry summer uncovered ridges never seen before and crevasses that previously had appeared to be smooth snow. Definite moraines laterally and at the terminal were found.

Salmon River, carrying much silt of the type scoured by ice, had been suspected of glacial origin but never before traced to one. T. Raymond Conway and Judge Fred W. Stadter, in planning a Mazama survey of Reid, recognized Palmer's glacial features as they crossed the exposed icefield. It lies below the mass called Triangle Moraine, so named for the Triangle YMCA climbers club, not its shape. The middle was crevassed heavily in 1924 and some fissures were deep. An arch of ice marked its terminal. Its length is about 4500 feet and the maximum width is 1/4-mile.

On Mount Hood's north slope, just west of Langille Crags between the lower parts of Eliot and Coe Glaciers is the remnant. In 1907 Sylvester called it an independent glacier and it appears on the USGS quadrangle map as a roughly circular icefield with one stream flowing into Coe branch of the Middle Fork.

Kenneth N. Phillips, a USGS associate engineer and chairman of the Mazama research committee, made a considerable study of this icefield. He reported that its glacial characteristics were apparent late in the summer of 1937. However, its shape has changed, a medial moraine having been built up to cleave the field in two sections. One lies below and offside of the larger upper one, while two tiny lakes now occupy hollows apparently formed by ice about 1907. The upper field is so steep as to require crampons for traverse. Presence of recently deposited morainal material and the discharge of water turbid with the scouring of the ice in its bed indicate that it still is a glacier, although dying fast. There is evidence that it once occupied much of the basin between Cloud Cap Inn and Coe Glacier. It lies between 7500 and 6500 feet elevation, 1000 feet of vertical difference between its top and terminus.

Kenneth Cameron and Pat Pringle, scientists of the USGS Cascades Volcano Observatory, Vancouver Washington, followed up the work of Phillips, who lives in Portland. They reported in 1989 that, in general, the Mount Hood glaciers have continued the slow process of melting. Some of them are receding faster than others. Zig Zag no longer extends as far as Crater Rock. Palmer has has shown no movement for several decades and "is probably classed as a permanent snow field."

18. Winter Climbing Begins

The race to be the first on top each year is an eagerly contested event. Prior to 1915 climbers were content to wait until the road to Government Camp was free of snow before beginning the annual march on the summit, but with more and more turning out each winter for skiing and snowshoeing, hardy Mazamas and others began casting eyes toward the peak and speculating on the possibility of winter ascents.

Although Charles E. Warner had yet to make his first climb of the peak, he and Elijah Coalman were first to climb in winter, and he cinched his record for all time at the end of that year by going up with the late William W. Evans and registering in the lookout cabin on New Year's day. Since then many climbers have struggled over ice and through blizzards, and one lost his life — in order to sign the book on January 1. But Warner, Coalman and Evans were the pioneers.

After an unsuccessful try on March 7 1915 with a party of Mazamas, their progress hampered by a tussle with heavy motion picture apparatus, Warner and Coalman remained over for a climb next day. The trail made the day before helped them and with fine weather conditions they reached the top. They climbed on snowshoes, although in places the surface was too icy for the webs. Coalman was surprised to see the Big Crevasse yawning to a width of 50 feet as it usually remains covered by snow until much later in the season. The record box was buried on Mazama Rock and they dug in the ice for an hour before being able to write that they had, on

March 8 1915 made the first winter climb.

The Christmas week following found T. Raymond Conway with Coalman at Cloud Cap Inn, set for a real dead-of-winter ascent. They tried Cooper's Spur on December 26 and 27, but were foiled by severe weather. They returned to Portland to accompany a Mazama New Year party on a skiing trip to the south side.

Enroute down from Cloud Cap they met Warner and Evans on the way up. Wearing fur parkas, they were well equipped for an Arctic-like expedition. They started for the summit early on the morning of December 31, and though weather conditions were good, deep, soft snow was encountered; much of the way they waded to their hips. When they reached the top at 4 pm, clouds had formed about the peak. They were forced to break into the newly completed cabin, and it probably saved their lives, for an intense storm raged that night. The oil stoves Coalman had taken up for heating and cooking purposes smoked badly and with snow banked deep around the walls and partially over the roof, the two adventurers nearly suffocated.

As soon as possible they started down the south side on the first day of 1916, in snow and dense fog. When this finally lifted sufficiently for them to get bearings, they were heading for Paradise Park, having drifted westerly across the snows below Crater Rock. Changing their course toward Government Camp they just had time to spot the hotel building far below when the storm resumed, and a high wind drove the flakes and sleet in sheets before them. Their parkas reached almost to their knees, and were much in the way as they sank deep in the soft snow.

The party of Mazamas at Government Camp had just finished dinner when they heard a voice calling from the forest above. Coalman, Conway and others, carrying lanterns, set out to lend aid. They soon found Evans, almost at the point of collapse, in snow to his waist, while Warner was almost a mile behind but in better physical condition. They were assisted to the hotel.

Warner had the bug badly, however, and with Coalman and four others he made a south side ascent on Washington's birthday following, a pleasant and uneventful experience under fine weather conditions when it was possible to use snowshoes all the way to the Big Crevasse.

Since then scarcely a year has gone that did not see names on the register, on or soon after each New Year's Day. With buildings at timberline available for shelter, an open road and ski trails, much of the hazard of mid-winter climbs is gone, and scores have been been making them. Not a few of the veterans include in their records ascents every month of the year. Skis, with sealskins, rope adjustments or climbing wax have made possible climbs to Crater Rock on the hickories, where they are left for a long speedy ride back down after the balance of the ascent is made afoot. Crampons, the hinged steel plates with long teeth for climbing on steep ice and hard snow are now in the kit of every winter climber. Woolen garments, plus light waterproof windbreakers, hip length and weighing less than a pound, have taken the place of the heavy fur-lined parkas of the early day crowd.

Many of the winter climbers hold that the going over a continuous snow trail is much easier than the summer ascents on alternate loose rock and snow, and that it is less exhausting than toiling along in the heat of the mid-summer sun. Crevasses are covered and there is little to fear in the hazard of avalanching. The high snow banks are carved into fantastic shapes by the action of the wind and sleet. Often, though, if the snow is frozen, these climbers have to chop steps from far below Crater Rock, a slow and tiresome job.

An ambitious pair ascending for New Year's day from Cloud Cap had to use their ice axes from the time they began ascending Cooper's Spur. Reaching the summit late in the day they found friends, who had made a leisurely trip up the south side under excellent conditions, signed up for the year's record hours ahead of the exhausted north-side climbers.

19. West Side Parks

Mount Hood's greatest charms are not seen by those who visit only the north and south sides. On the west side are vistas of unmatched grandeur. Great glaciers, particularly the cascading Reid, extend down to the meadowed parklands, and their streams own deep canyons. Above and beside these glaciers the mountain's sternest battlements of rock offer climbers problems of skill and endurance. Waterfalls plunge over the steps of lava bench.

Graceful alpine firs and black hemlock, with drooping leaders bobbing in the breeze, are clumped in the meadows. They line the low hummocks about the timberline parks in landscaping schemes that no man can emulate. In the meadows, some as velvety as city lawns, flow murmuring rills of ice-cold water, product of the higher snowbanks. Marmot lookouts whistle their limpid, round warning from posts beside their warrens in the boulder slopes; the unique call of the Clark nutcracker echoes through the forest. Flowers carpet the meadows from snow until snow.

Because of isolation the west side for many years had few visitors. Deep canyons and lofty ridges separate it from the other sections, but a greater impediment than these natural obstacles to public enjoyment has been Portland's Bull Run Watershed. When this reserve was created 50 years ago and made inviolate to all public entry, it included a township which reaches up the slopes of Mount Hood itself. Despite general belief — built up by enthusiasm for the city's fine water — no part of the supply comes from Mount Hood. The Bull Run Watershed is fed by springs and heavy winter snowfall. A glance at any good map will show its isolation from the mountain.

Water melting from the snowbanks and glaciers on Mount Hood's westerly slopes flows into the tributaries of two streams, the west fork of Hood River, and the Sandy River system. The Sandy flows in a semi-circle around the east, south and west sides of the Bull Run basin, the latter stream then entering the Sandy to the west. High ridges surround the basin — even from them creeks feed the Sandy and the Hood — so it is plain Portland gets none of its water supply from Mount Hood.

The township mentioned lies entirely outside the Bull Run drainage, and no one seems to know why it was included in the reserve. But it is there, sacrosanct by Act of Congress, barring any road or trail, construction through it to the most beautiful region in Oregon.

Mountain enthusiasts would not be denied forever, so they began visiting it by ways that remained open. There being no road across Lolo Pass, they attained Eden Park and Wy'east Basin by trails from the Hood River valley and Cloud Cap, or via another trail from the south at timberline over the west side of the mountain. This is part of the Forest Service's bridle and footpath around the mountain. Paradise Park, below the Zig Zag Glacier, is reached by a fine trail from Twin Bridges on the Loop Highway below Laurel hill, or via the Timberline Trail.

This has been changed. Lolo Pass Road was built, linking to the road between Hood River and Lost Lake. The footpath became the Timberline Trail circling the Mountain.

Public attention has been drawn to these parks in recent years. The Oregon Nature Lovers' Club, of Hood River, explored the region in 1922 and gave its features fanciful names. The area below Ladd Glacier and Barrett Spur became "Wy'east Basin Park;" the adjoining ridge, "Vista," and the beautiful section between Eden and Cathedral Ridges became "Eden Park."

In the same year John A. Lee and Richard W. Montague, Mazama leaders, began a campaign to open Paradise Park. Simon Benson furnished half the funds for building the park trail, and the Forest Service built a better path from the north by Tony Creek.

With 36 Mazamas, Lee that year led the first climb from Paradise Park to the summit.

Paradise Park became so popular that agitation began for a road from the Loop highway, but that was barred by the Bull Run boundary. Opposition also arose to marring the primitive scene with highway scars. All possibility of a road to the west side was eliminated by placing the area in the Mount Hood Wilderness.

20. Disaster on Coe Glacier

On the north side of Mount Hood there was more than usual to interest the crowd at Cloud Cap Inn, Sunday, July 17 1927. The sky was without a cloud, no haze hung over the walls above the glaciers, the lookout cabin on top was plainly in view, even a few climbers from the south side could be seen strolling about.

On Cooper's Spur were climbing parties, while others crossed Eliot Glacier, visiting the seracs and the crevasses. Most eyes were drawn, however, to a scene high on the face of the peak, far over to the right where big mountaineering business was under way. For arm-chair climbers a view of people struggling up a mountainside is ever fascinating, and all the telescopes and binoculars available were in use.

The center of interest was a long, thin line of humanity, black against the steep snow of upper Coe Glacier, crawling toward the northwest arete. The snow was soft; progress was slow because many in the string were having their first experience in high work. A typical well-organized Mazama climbing party was in action — a procession of 103 men and women, roped in parties of about 10 each. Watchers could see the individual figures of men ahead, at the sides and in the rear, veteran mountain guides assuring that the squads kept safely in line.

Judge Stadter, president of the club that year, was leader on this, the annual Mount Hood climb, staged as nearly as possible on the club's birthday. They were traversing from the American Legion camp near Cloud Cap Inn over the top to Government

Camp, for a dinner planned at 4 PM. Families of some in the party were watching from the Inn, a few were exchanging heliograph signals.

Suddenly one of the watchers screamed as the climbing line broke, the third squad high up plunging down the mountain. Bedlam broke loose as the climbers attempted to stay their slide. They seemed to skid crazily downward, first one end, then the other, then the middle, as individuals strove to check their fall by digging into the snow with alpenstocks. In a few seconds, the mass of humanity, arms, legs, packs, equipment tossed about and disappeared over a wall of ice.

The horrified watchers saw the guides hurrying down the slope, heedless of their own safety, to the brink of the crevasse, then disappear. Others cast off ropes and descended, until it seemed half the party had left the climbing trail.

Serious though this accident was, still greater tragedy was averted by almost miraculous circumstance. When the first 10 slid from the trail they sped toward a large crevasse in the angle where the line of slope changed slightly. The upper lip of the crevasse overhung the vertical upper wall. The impetus of the victims and this overhang threw them, after a fall of perhaps 20 feet, from the lip into soft snow on a bench beyond the lower brink of the chasm. The bottom in some places was estimated at 100 feet from the surface. Had these hapless climbers slid over the cliff more slowly, it is doubtful any would have survived.

This is what happened in the line: The climbers were on the steepest snow of their entire route — a stretch of possibly 1000 feet which was considered a marked hazard. A few minutes before, a small avalanche had knocked one man off his feet. No one was injured but it was suggested that this may have unnerved some of the climbers. The line then paused for a brief rest.

All the climbers were tied together. They carried alpenstocks which they dug into the snow on the upward side of the trail as they made the steep traverse. Someone in the middle slipped. The leader of the string said he suddenly felt a sharp tug on the rope about his waist and was yanked from the trail. That jerk was great enough to snatch loose the alpenstocks of some. Others hung on and tried desperately to brake the terrific plunge. Some spread-eagled on the snow, others dug in their heels. Nothing worked. The angle of the slope was too steep and too many were in the party, tied together close as they were, to resist the involuntary glissade down the steep incline.

A grievous scene was there in the soft snow for the rescuers. who dashed down almost as rapidly as the others fell down. Clem Blakney, an assisting guide who had taken many parties to the top, was the first to arrive. From the gory tangle he pulled Mary Malloy, whose right ankle had a compound fracture. Nearby lay Dr. Stanton W. Stryker, a Portland dentist, his body pierced through with an alpenstock; Blakney dragged him free and drew out the alpenstock. Two small sleds, brought by the climbers to slide down the south side, were used instead by the injured. And stretchers were rigged from alpenstocks, coats and pack sacks.

The difficult task of carrying the injured off the glaciers was not completed until late afternoon. Dr. Stryker was carried only a half-mile when he lost consciousness and died. Seven others were taken to hospitals. Mazamas at Cloud Cap organized the rescue work, summoning doctors and nurses from Hood River. The Crag Rats, a Hood River mountaineering and rescue group, won high praise for participating. A score of them were on the glacier preparing for a ski tournament and saw the mishap. They hastened over, brought a stretcher and first aid kits, and joined in bringing down the injured.

Meanwhile, those remaining high up on the trail, who could not go to the aid of the injured, reorganized and climbed across the summit and down to Government Camp.

The Mazamas, in an inquiry after the accident, found that every effort had been made toward a "safe" climb. Judge Stadter had scouted the route the week before with H. K. Sieke and Charles Wilson. This was the first time the club had planned an ascent over the Sunshine Trail. Stadter said the scouts found the trail dangerous in the upper glacier but it could be made with caution, and so it was decided to go that way.

One-fourth of this large party had had no previous climbing experience, so the leaders had taken great pains to avert mishap. They inspected boots and climbing equipment. They gave full instructions in footwork and use of the rope. The one factor that can never be eliminated in any such enterprise, they pointed out, is human reaction. Leaders of large climbing parties devote more thought to personnel than any other phase of planning. When all mechanical problems have been solved, the personal factor remains a concern until the last climber returns to camp.

Soon after this accident the club formed a permanent committee to examine the whole technique of climbing. This committee made exhaustive studies of clothing, equipment, food, physical factors, temperament, and methods of solving the many problems of rock and snow ascent. Mazamas made good use of their findings.

The term safety, when used for a mountain climb, is relative. On no peak worth going after is risk absent. But if climbing were freed of this, zest would be lost from the sport and, for many, the incentive for mountaineering with it.

21. The Hunt Goes On

On a south side climb in 1936 a veteran of many seasons on the mountain paused at Crater Rock, looked down the snowfields and asked, "I wonder where Brownlee is, down there?"

Since New Years Day 1927, hardly a climbing party has gone that way without someone asking the same question. On the trail, at the inns, around campfires, in the dilapidated cabin on the summit, the tragedy was discussed. Leslie Brownlee, of Portland, age 21, yielded his life in the effort to be, with his companion, the first to make the ascent that year. His story was discussed countless times over many years.

Skiers, hikers, mountain workers often took time out as they traversed that slope to peer into crevasses and climb over rocks hoping to find a clue that will help clear up the mystery. Hope lingered long among his relatives and friends and the hundreds who engaged in the desperate, prolonged quest for him, that the rocks and glaciers some day would reveal his ultimate fate.

Brownlee and Al Feyerabend, a school friend, planned to enter their names in the peak's record book on that New Year Day. They had made the climb several times. On the Friday night before, at Battle Ax Inn, Government Camp, they were ready to go. Skies were overcast but temperatures were above freezing and others had left for the summit under similar weather conditions. They were equipped with snowshoes for the deep snow, parkas, flashlights for the night journey through the forest, hot food in flasks to sustain themselves.

They reached the Camp Blossom cabin at 1:30 am, and began the try for the summit one hour later. The next afternoon Feyerabend returned to that cabin alone. Brownlee has not been seen since.

In Feyerabend's written account, he said it remained clear enough as late as 4 am for them to see the lights of Portland. An hour later they were in a heavy storm but they struggled on until 6 o'clock when drowsiness overtook them and they lay down in the snow and slept. On awakening they were so cold they were barely able to pick up their packs and go on. It was snowing heavily and there was little visibility, but they continued the effort. Working to the right, they went to the brink of White River Glacier and ascended the moraine at its head.

They expected then to encounter the steep slope at the base of Crater Rock but did not, so they began working westward again. Later they tried a compass course due north, hoping it would lead to the Rock. Soon afterward, Feyerabend wrote, Brownlee showed signs of exhaustion. He decided to turn back, taking the compass and setting a course that would return him to the highway. But despite the snow and zero visibility Feyerabend continued toward the summit, fearing ridicule if he failed, as both had promised friends they would be "first up" in 1927. The effort proved too much for him, and he too gave up, not knowing his high point of advance except that it was below Crater Rock.

Beset by whirling snow and biting wind which roared across the high wastes, and staggering with exhaustion through the soft mass with every step, Feyerabend had a close brush with death. He wandered a good deal but, fortunately, at a most opportune moment for safety, the clouds lifted and he saw the cliffs of Mississippi Head, the great rock that rears at the head of the Zig Zag Canyon trough. He realized he was following the course that has led many to disaster — they drift with the westward tilt below Crater Rock. He cut sharply to the right and finally reached Camp Blossom.

There he found that four youths had just gone down toward Government Camp and he assumed one of them was Brownlee.

Meanwhile, a hunt had started for another youth, Calvin White Jr., lost in the forest above Government Camp. With two others on skis, they became tired and started to return when White raced on ahead, but then failed to reach Government Camp. Now rescuers took on the added search for Brownlee. Literally every possible agency was called in — Mazamas, Crag Rats, Trails Club, student hiking clubs, Portland police, and deputy sheriffs of four counties. Loggers, forest rangers, other woodsmen and hardy crews who worked with them turned out by dozens, even tough timber cruisers, combing assigned sections of the wilderness.

From a sickbed rose T. Raymond Conway, an expert on the paths, habits and moods of Mount Hood, to take charge of the advanced search headquarters at Camp Blossom. On a battered woodstove food and drink were stewed and brewed, with empty cans as cooking vessels. The dilapidated bunks were occupied night and day as weary searchers, their energies spent, stumbled in to sleep. The Forest Service ran a telephone line to keep contact between Blossom and the Battle Ax Inn at Government Camp.

In general command was L. A. Nelson, lumber technician, mountain climber and explorer, chosen because of his leadership qualities. With scarcely an hour of sleep in a week, he worked through the bedlam of the Battle Ax to run an orderly, thorough, progressive search. For a week Manager Everett Sickler turned over the little hotel to Nelson. Husky men, gaunt, numbed by cold and fatigue and frost-bite, sick from the arduous grind over soft, deep snow, their clothes watersoaked, stomped into the building and fell to the floor if they did not find a seat. From antlers of mounted animal heads, from racks and Indian and pioneer relics on display in the lobby, dripping garments hung; before the roaring fireplace, steaming boots dried.

Mountain guides Lije Coalman and Mark Weygandt joined, as did John A. Lee and Eugene H. Dowling, noted for leading summit climbers in parties of hundreds. On the list of groups that Nelson methodically dispatched from the hurly burly of the Inn were practically every noted climber in the Northwest.

No faintest clue was disregarded. When it was suggested the storm had driven both youths far eastward, a party started for the highway bridge to check the White River Canyon. Deep tracks, obviously new, were traced out to a trapper. Money, supplies and equipment arrived from Portland. And snowshoes — the day of travel by skis had not yet arrived — came by the dozens. At timberline between 40 and 50 inches of new snow fell that week, covering every and any mark young Brownlee might have left. His mother, quartered at Government Camp Hotel, kept a room ready for the son she confidently expected would return alive. A Portland banker drove up and down the highway all night, flashing his searchlight as a beacon.

It was accepted that Brownlee had not gone above Crater Rock, so this was the apex of a search triangle, with the highway as base, the White River Bridge to the east and the outlet of Zig Zag Canyon as the angles. This large region, all of it rough and steep and more than two-thirds heavily timbered, was parceled out with prominent landmarks as division places, and separate groups combed these sections one by one. When the storm finally let up and a howling east wind brought clear skies and bitter cold, they searched the region around Crater Rock, paying close attention to the hot spots which were bare of snow — on the slim chance that Brownlee might have got there.

Not the remotest clue was found.

Fate was in happier mood for Calvin White. Although lightly clad, without food, he was known to have gone below timberline. It was fairly certain he had drifted westward where canyons would keep him from moving any great distance from Government Camp. Still, no trace was found until Monday morning, after he had been out three nights. Bill Lenz, a Tarzan-like woodsman, trailing with Dick Scott, detected faint ski tracks leading to a small flat on the west side of the Little Zig Zag River, several miles north and west of Government Camp.

Above Lenz and Scott on the other side of the stream, Crag Rats Kent Shoemaker, William Hukari and Paul Hoerlein also followed the tracks to the Little Zig Zag. There the skier had sat down and slid into the creek basin. He had crossed and continued, floundering through deep snow. Then his tracks disappeared. This information was relayed to headquarters.

Another Crag Rat, William Cochran of Hood River, left the Battle Ax, picked up the tracks and was able to trace them to a spot where White had made a bed of fir boughs, then had stumbled along without skis. The trail was hot.

Cochran knew the youth, or his body, was close. He shouted. Calvin White called back in a weak voice. In a little place sheltered by a rock and a fallen tree, Cochran found the youth, so
weak that he could not move. The spot was 2-1/2 miles from Government Camp.

Removing White's sodden, freezing clothing, Cochran took
the warm dry garments from his own back and re-dressed the
youth. He gave him warm water and started for assistance. His revolver shots soon brought others. A sled was made of skis, warm
clothes added and he was taken to a toboggan, while a messenger
went off to notify search headquarters.

Earl Hammond, Alaskan explorer who had been at Government Camp with a husky dog team for winter sports, rushed out
with 20 men on snowshoes breaking trail. A bed had been prepared on the sled, lined with hot water bags. Night had fallen and
flares were lighted far up the trail. Intense excitement prevailed.
Searchers, highway officers, residents and visitors, the crowd num-
bering many hundreds, gathered at the Inn. Waiting newsreel cam-
eramen set up their machines. Brownlee's mother, a registered
nurse stood by, ready for the battle to save his life.

Soon, far up the mountainside, the dogs were heard barking
as the sled clattered behind. Hammond spurred them on. Then
they appeared on the last pitch above the highway, Hammond
braking hard against the excited dash of the dogs. Many persons
were crying as the sled drew to a stop and the thin white face of
the boy was revealed as his father embraced him. Quickly he was
carried to the room where doctor and nurse went to work. Calvin
was taken to Portland the next day. He recovered, although it was
necessary to amputate the tips of two of his frozen toes.

White had done something that is very easy for inexperienced
travelers descending from Camp Blossom — he followed the westward dip of the land into the basin of the Little Zig Zag. His trail
indicated he had never left that small valley in his wanderings.

After a week the intensive search for Brownlee ended. Nelson and Conway held a conference with all hands and agreed that
everything possible had been done. Ten men, including Coalman
and Weygandt, remained at Camp Blossom. Later the group was
reduced to four. On January 8 Weygandt and Lenz climbed to the

summit, after cutting steps in the ice for 2000 feet. They found the cabin buried in 8 feet of ice. In that long struggle Lenz froze a finger. In April, when the snow began to disappear, Lenz searched again. Nelson and Conway had pledged to comb the entire mountainside at the height of warm summer weather. They did that with 78 men participating, on August 26. No clue was found.

A dog "detective" named Arnold von Winkelreid was taken on another hunt the same month. The dog found a camera, packsacks, gloves and other climbers' gear; none linked with Brownlee.

Afterward, theory upon theory was built, explored and dumped. The youth had been well clothed, wore a wind-breaking parka, carried an ice ax, dark glasses, compass and a packsack with food in a thermos flask. These were materials that in part, at least, would withstand the ravages of severe weather even after his mortal remains vanished. Somewhere on Mount Hood's southern fields of rock and ice, if he did not fall into a crevasse and carry them with him, these identifying objects remain.

22. The Deadly Fumarole

The strangest tragedy of Mount Hood climbing history was due to the fact that the peak is a volcano and the effect of its fires still linger. The gases from the fumaroles high on the peak are deadly [for lack of oxygen], if enough are inhaled. Of the thousands who have made the climb through the old crater, few can say they have not smelled the pungent vapors that can be seen steaming from the vents. Many, indeed, have been sickened, some so they could not continue the ascent above Crater Rock.

Victor F. von Norman, age 22, student at the University of Washington, whose curiosity lured him into one of the highest and largest of the fumaroles, became a victim of a noxious gas so concentrated that the cavern he entered held no oxygen. In the work to recover his body, two men were rendered unconscious, seven others were seriously affected, and a half-dozen more at the cave's mouth suffered too.

In attempting to recover von Norman's body, rescuers were forced to use oxygen helmets. The most improved types of army gas masks, containing chemicals that remove poisonous fumes from the air, proved useless here. The spectacle was presented, too, of members of a metropolitan fire department laboriously climbing a high mountain for a rescue.

Von Norman was with four men touring mountain peaks in the Northwest. They climbed to the summit of Mount Hood August 27 1934 over the south side route, traversing the snow wedge of the hogsback and ascending the wall beyond. While on the hogsback returning, he decided to look into the steaming vent where the snow and ice lie against the north face of Crater Rock — at nearly 11,000 feet elevation. With Edward Tremper he left the climbing trail to step over to the opening. One side of this cave is the volcanic structure of the Rock, the other ice. The warm vapor discharging from the rock had melted out the cavern, which descended at a steep angle under the ice cap.

Von Norman entered, with Tremper about 20 feet behind. They had gone about 60 feet, Tremper said, when von Norman stopped abruptly and turned back, showing signs of extreme distress. He scrambled upward a few feet, then faltered, reeled and dropped to the bottom of the pit — nearly 200 feet down. Tremper, also suffering from the gas, went back and called to the others.

A quarter of a mile away and several hundred feet below, Aunnie Faubion and Harold Taylor, of the Forest Service, were at work building a shelter house east of Crater Rock. The climbers hurried over to ask for aid. Faubion, a native of the Mount Hood country, took all the pack rope he had and went to the vent. At the opening he took off his shirt, soaked it in snow water, bound it about his face, and with a rope securely attached to his waist, asked two others to lower him into the hole. The attempt failed. The rope was too short and Faubion was sickened by the gas. Taylor attempted to go down but he too was overcome. He was dragged out in hysterical condition and had to be restrained from dashing back in.

Faubion then dispatched a runner to summon help at a lookout station just above timberline. Leaving Taylor and the others at Crater Rock he too rushed with his pack horses down to the lookout station. From there Paul and Bob Williams, and Ralph Olson, a fireman, started for the crater with lights and other equipment, and two gas masks.

Paul Williams and Olson both went far into the cave wearing gas masks but found them useless for lack of air to breathe. Both suffered severely from the fumes. Others continued the attempt without success. Olson returned below to telephone for oxygen equipment, the only means possible to recover the body.

Meanwhile the state police had flashed news of the accident to Portland and a rescue unit of the Portland fire department was

The Hogsback climbing hazard below Crater Rock, 1947;
von Norman died in fumarole below left (chapter 22). Mt.
Jefferson at top left

Wy'east has a thousand faces — Squaw grass adorns ridge below Mt. Hood, 1931

Timberline Lodge opened for business in 1938 — Wy'east has a thousand faces

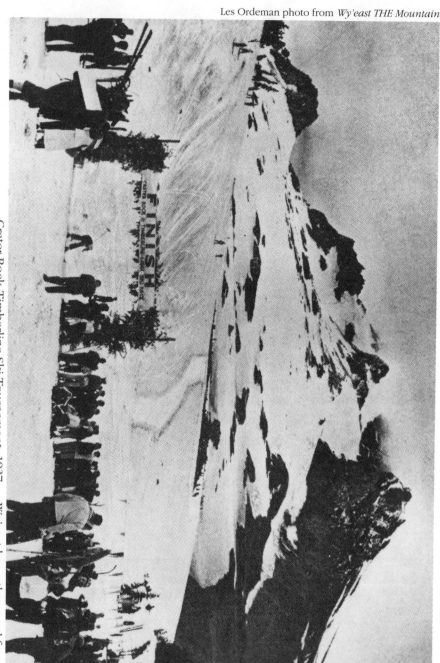

Crater Rock-Timberline Ski Tournament, 1937 — Wy'east has a thousand faces

In 1937, 22-foot snowfall buried timberline "hotel" up to eaves, forcing entry through attic, thence down ladder inside

Wy'east has a thousand faces — lone climber on Eliot Glacier

Photo © George M. Henderson

Ski Jumping Tourney Judges, 1937: from left, Harold Lee, Fred Van Dyke, Peter Hostmark, Earl Little and Fred H. McNeil

Moon over Mount Hood west side, 1955 — Wy'east has a thousand faces

Wy'east has a thousand faces — climbers resting at Barrett Spur

Photo © David Falconer

Built in 1889, Cloud Cap Inn has weathered a century

Disabled ski meet, Mt. Hood Meadows

Rock shelter, McNeil Point — Wy'east has a thousand faces

Skiing the highest levels at Mount Hood Meadows

Timberline Lodge in midwinter — Wy'east has a thousand faces

Snowshoes and skis modeled by Jim Harlow and Al Monner, 1930

Wy'east has a thousand faces — Seracs in Eliot Glacier, Ray Atkeson viewing

Lookout cabin on top Mount Hood, after 1921 storm

Skiers near Illumination Rock, 1964

A busy day at Ski Bowl, Multorpor Mountain, 1947

On Timberline Trail crossing Cathedral Ridge below McNeil Point — Wy'east has a thousand faces

J. Frank Drake and climbing party at Government Camp, about 1892

Climbing party on summit, with "Ranger" and "Laddie," 1930

Sarah "Tantsana" Langille, on porch of Cloud Cap Inn, 1892

The "modern" loop highway on east side Mount Hood, July 1929

Death in fumarole – top: mouth of cavern where von Norman died – center: hauling out body by rope – bottom: moving body by tobaggan

Top: In months shifting ice ruined shelter above White River Glacier – Bottom: Kenneth Phillips and J. Russell Collins sampled fumaroles, 1935

Lije Coalman, lower right, lived in tent while building fire lookout tower, Mt. Hood summit, 1915. Left, Coalman and George Ledford

Anna Strong crossing Big Crevasse, 1915, via Lije
Coalman's rickety ladder, aided by Kan Smith

Cloud Cap Inn guests rode all day in "democrat wagon" up from Hood River train station, 1893

The "ghost forest" near Coe Glacier, 1938

Part of 1947 American Legion climbing party (Crag Rats in checkered shirts)

dispatched. It carried oxygen-breathing helmets, Gibbs masks and two all-service masks, and a large quantity of rope. With siren wailing, the firemen made the run from the city to the end of the road at timberline in less than two hours. From there up they took equipment on Faubion's horses.

Captain F. W. Roberts led the fire crew in this novel high altitude rescue, along with firemen C. M. Ferris and E. R. Hornschuh, and the Clackamas County Coroner Arnold Bierman. At the scene ropes were tied on two men wearing the oxygen helmets. Reaching the bottom, they found the body wedged tightly between the rocks and the snow wall in a narrow opening. They had trouble getting a rope around the body. Encumbered as they were, the strenuous work forced them to retreat. Paul Williams then returned and freed the body, steering it up the slope as many hands above hauled it to the surface. It was carried to timberline on a horse.

All who entered the cavern suffered from the fumes. Williams and Gary Leach, of Government Camp, were hauled out unconscious. The firemen, already tired by their rush to this high altitude effort, were forced to resuscitate these men. Oxygen was given to several others who had faced the terrible gas in the pit. Williams was taken to a hospital suffering intense chest pain and barely able to breathe. Leach, while not gassed so severely, was almost blind. He too required hospital treatment.

The firemen themselves had trouble breathing. Captain Roberts said they detected no other gases at the vent but sulfur. "But that was plenty strong — sickening in fact. It was a peculiar experience. I went down a little way and was affected. I was all right when I looked straight ahead but if I turned my head in the slightest, right or left, everything went black. I can well understand why this lad suddenly toppled over and fell."

What were the gases that caused the death of von Norman and have sickened others who passed through the crater? The question whether Mount Hood remains a live volcano, or whether its fires are dead, has been a topic of discussion since white men began settling the valleys about it.

It is common, especially in cold winter months, to see steam around Crater Rock. The white clouds sometimes ascend in quantities sufficient to partly obscure the summit. When wind currents are favorable, the sulfurous reek has been noticed at Government Camp and at the highway crossing of White River, more than 10 miles from the crater. Aviators who have flown around the summit also have smelled the gases.

Sylvester, in a widely quoted *National Geographic* article in 1908, discussed what he considered evidence of increasing activity in the fumaroles about the crater. This received wide attention but there is no evidence that any attempt was made to verify his findings. The von Norman tragedy revived interest in the question and, 27 years after Sylvester's examination, research was instituted and it is hoped, will be continued.

So far as climbers can ascertain, all the active fumaroles but one are now within the crater. Those who have reached the summit by the Steel's Cliff route report finding one steaming away on the top of that promontory. Below it are a large number sending up vapor to attract the notice of those who pass by. In some years the fumaroles appear more active than others, governed, it is thought, by the amount of snowfall. Many accounts by climbers indicate the fumaroles were much more active in the 19th Century.

The incessant avalanching of the brittle wall also exposes new vents for escape of gases, at the same time carrying away others. The fumes are always noticeable, and seem to be more disagreeable when relative humidity is higher.

During an ascent in August 1867 an immense fissure was found in the old crater, an estimated 300 feet from the summit — possibly the "Big Crevasse" of later years — from which came puffs of sulfurous smoke and a hissing sound, "like boiling."

Oliver Yocum led a climb in August 1896 when the vents about Crater Rock were said to have "smoked and steamed constantly" and "by applying the ear to the ground, boiling and sputtering of water could be heard distinctly." In that party, Eugene White, of Portland, wrote that "by digging away the loose volcanic earth and rock, an egg could be cooked or coffee boiled by placing the pot or can in the excavation and replacing the earth about it."

What is a fumarole? In their 1935 account in the *Mazama Annual*, Kenneth Phillips and J. Russell Collins reviewed the club's preliminary study. They defined it as derived from the diminutive of the Latin "fumarium" (smoke chamber), or little chimney — commonly, a vent in the ground from which gases of volcanic origin discharge. Common usage, these writers explain, extends the meaning to include volcanic vapors. A volcano, in its period of quiescence, may be considered a great fumarole or a group of fumaroles. The surface of a liquid stream of lava acts as an immense and active fumarole, discharging large quantities of dry, white fumes at high temperatures. As the lava cools these give way to gases composed of hydrochloric or sulfurous acid, with water vapor, which issue at a lower temperature.

In a still later stage the vents emit sulfur or hydrogen sulfide with large amounts of water vapor and, usually, carbon dioxide. Methane (marsh gas) carbon monoxide and atmospheric air are often present. Sulfur dioxide may occur but not along with hydrogen sulfide because these two gases react to form new compounds. A vent in this stage may be properly termed a "solfatura," after a classic example near Naples, Italy.

In the final stage the fumarole weakly discharges water vapor alone or a little carbon dioxide. A vent of this type is sometimes known as a "Mofette," the transition to which, from an active volcano, may require many centuries.

Many of the Mount Hood fumaroles are at inaccessible spots on the cliffs. Others, under the snow, because of their heat, produce caverns. The Mazamas selected and marked four of the more accessible vents for study — listed here as A, B, C and D.

Fumarole A, consisting of a number of small vents called by climbers the Devil's Kitchen, is 125 feet southwest of the shelter hut in the saddle above White River Glacier. The gases have encrusted the openings with yellow, white and greenish sublimations. The crust was found to be warm over an area 30 feet in diameter, even where there was no apparent gas discharge. With a sound like escaping steam, the gases were found pouring from the vents, and smelled strongly of hydrogen sulfide.

Thermometers in the vents registered 192-194 degrees F, the average being the exact boiling point of water at that elevation, 10,200 feet. Temperatures were the same in observations a month later. In three other small vents nearby, identical temperature was recorded.

Heavy condensation on a cold metal plate indicated water vapor was a chief constituent of the gas. Bright or plated metal was stained black at once. The red lead paint on an alpenstock turned black. Litmus tests gave a weak acid reaction and lead acetate paper became black, showing presence of hydrogen sulfide, hence, the absence of sulfur dioxide. The silver nitrate test for chlorides could not be made as the hydrogen sulfide created a silver sulfide precipitate which became black quickly. A glass plate exposed to the fumes for two hours was not etched, so hydrofluoric acid was not present in quantity.

A specimen of oxalated blood in a tube was the means of a test for carbon monoxide when the gas was passed through it. The blood gradually became darker, almost black, largely due to the action of carbon dioxide which changed the bright arterial blood to venous blood. Any measurable amount of carbon monoxide would have turned the blood a bright cherry red. This blood was later examined at the University of Oregon Medical School by Joseph Beeman, who reported a test for carbon monoxide was negative. He found a trace of hydrogen sulfide but no cyanide.

Fumarole B, a large vertical vent on top of Crater Rock, is at an elevation of 10,300 feet. Water vapor mixed with air emerged in a vigorous current. No sublimates were found around this vent and no sulfurous odor. The temperature four feet below the surface was 160 degrees. The gas reaction was weakly acid, but hydrogen sulfide was absent. Carbon dioxide was present in much less concentration than in fumarole A.

Fumarole C is an open vertical vent south of B on the same ridge. Moss grew up to its opening and water vapor and air were issuing. There was no noticeable odor and the temperature, four feet inside, was 120 degrees.

Fumarole D, examined in October, is 400 feet northeast of the shelter hut at the base of Steel's cliff, at about 10,300 feet. A large volume of gas was emanating almost horizontally with great force from under a boulder covered with sublimed sulfur. Lead sulfide showed in a test and the hydrogen sulfide was strong. The gas appeared to be chiefly water vapor.

Samples of fumarole gases were analyzed by the chemistry department of Reed College. In the 1936 *Mazama Annual* Phillips discussed the results. Commenting on men who were overcome by the gas, the writer said they contained less than one per cent oxygen, hence von Norman suffocated, and the others were overcome by the toxic hydrogen sulfide.

In summary these investigators held that no explosive eruption of the volcano may be expected. The fumaroles seem to be safety valves releasing steam which might otherwise cause destruction. They pose no danger so long as climbers stay in the open air. Instead, wrote Phillips, in many respects the fumaroles are more interesting than the climb beyond to the summit.

In 1988 Kenneth Cameron, geologist of the Cascades Volcano Observatory, Vancouver, Washington, surveyed the fumaroles. He found the hot areas much larger than McNeil's description. Just under the ground surface, Cameron wrote, are crystalline sulfur deposits. The small lake near the Coalman Glacier has disappeared, leaving a 30-ft. deep hole.

23. The Zig Zag Mud River

Portland residents often have been excited by what they believed was the sight of smoke plumes rising above the summit of Mount Hood and blowing in the wind. One of the greatest such thrills occurred in August 1921 when word was telephoned that an eruption was pouring a flow of hot lava down the south side!

It was said the stream carried hot water and volcanic sand mixed with boulders...a mass so warm that geologists could not go near...spreading fanwise over the snowfields and clouds of steam rising...a red glare had been seen at the base of Crater Rock in the night...there had been an earthquake.

Tales like these, relayed from Government Camp, had people goggle-eyed. Not long before, they had heard of an enormous slide on Mount Adams descending a vertical mile over two glaciers and spreading over an area of 6000 acres, and had been ascribed by some to seismic action. Now Mount Hood was doing the same.

It did not take long to shake the bottom out of these wild reports. Orval Zimmerman and Chester Treichel, Government Camp guides, ascertained quickly that the flow was not hot. Indeed it was a narrow ribbon of mud streaming from a crack in the Zig Zag Glacier below Crater Rock. Nevertheless, the phenomenon was one of the most interesting Mount Hood had shown since white men began settling there. It has occurred before and since; in 1937 a much more extensive slide over the head of the Sandy Glacier was even visible from Portland.

In 1921 Clem Blakney, the summit lookout, spent a nervous night in the quivering cabin while great slides roared into the crater below. They probably were connected with the mud flow farther down. The slides swept away the climbing lifeline above the Big Crevasse and tore out telephone wires. A. Boyd Williams and T. Raymond Conway investigated and found that a tremendous force had lifted and cracked the upper end of the Zig Zag Glacier for 100 yards. The mass poured through a gap 40 feet long and 20 inches wide. The action shattered the ice about this fissure and humped huge blocks of it 4 feet above the surface.

In reporting for the Mazamas, Williams and Conway found no indication of explosive action. The flow was about 50 feet wide below the opening and extended 2100 feet down the glacier where much dropped into a crevasse. They advanced various theories that water had flown over or under the glacier and caused the slides. Climbers had often heard water running under the glacier, and so believed the chute in which it lies is a water course in summer, and an ice stream bed in winter. There was no indication that the volcano's internal heat caused this event.

Alleged "smoke" plumes often are realistic but they usually are composed of fine dry snow scooped up and swept by the wind over the summit. The steep walls of the crater and the long narrow chute west of Crater Rock combine to form strong drafts like a tall chimney. This pulls dry powder snow up over the top in a grand display. The same is seen from another cause — fog or low-lying clouds in this furious wind stream; this collects in the crater, then rises and pours up through the Zig Zag trough, boiling out like smoke in a seeming "eruption."

There is no authentic record, however, of smoke or vapors of fumaroles rising densely enough to be visible from Portland.

One W. F. Courtney, of Walla Walla, said he was camped in Tygh Valley in 1859 when he saw a smoke cloud rising in daytime, followed that night by a display of flames on the peak. But Arnold Hague wrote that "no eruption of Mount Hood can have taken place within a very long time — certainly not within the memory of man." And S. F. Emmons, writing for the American Geographic Society, reassured Portlander that "any return of activity would be heralded long in advance by floods cause by the melting of snow and ice fields," as heat surged up in the cone.

The famous Sylvester report, "Is Our Noblest Volcano Awakening to New Life?" based on a 1907 mapping expedition of the Mount Hood quadrangle said Steel's cliff showed more steam than usual. On August 28, men climbing to the east slope from Government Camp told him they had observed a column of "smoke," probably dense steam, rising high about the summit all day. Many others at Government Camp saw it too, and it was reported from points in the Willamette valley.

That night, from Government Camp a glow was seen behind crater Rock, "like a chimney burning out." and the White River rose to an angry stream three times its previous volume. Sylvester saw no reason for a rise except for an increase in volcanic heat as the weather then was cold and cloudy, and no possibility of glacial melting from the sun.

These phenomena occurred at a time that changes were being observed in the Bogoslof group of volcanic islands off the coast of Alaska, and Sylvester believed they were somehow associated. Mount Hood, he concluded, must be taken from the list of extinct volcanoes and placed among the doubtful.

In 1896 a climbing accident was blamed on volcanic activity when Fay Killingsworth was nearly killed by a falling boulder near the Big Crevasse. The rock bounced over her head but a spurt of snow threw her 50 feet downhill into a crevasse. She was rescued without great injury.

But members of the party smelled sulfurous vapor and "smoke and steam rising issuing from a towering cliff directly above." The girl's father, William Killingsworth, said an "eruption" caused the accident. This was disputed by Will Steel, who blamed an inexperienced guide for crossing dangerous avalanche channels; he held that any man who knew the mountain would have avoided it.

Killingsworth denounced Steel's implications and retorted in a letter, "While others may prefer a vacation spent in climbing Mount Hood, visiting a crater that is by no means extinct, and inhaling sulfurous fumes and risking life, limb and health in the effort, as for me and mine, we will hereafter be content with more rational, if more insipid recreations."

The public was told emphatically that it is dangerous to climb past Crater Rock without a guide. Said the *The Oregonian* in a ponderous editorial:

"There is no objection to mountain climbing as a recreation for an adventurous party of pleasure-seekers when the summit of the mountain chosen for the experiment is relatively easy of access, but the ascent of the steeper acclivities and more lofty peaks of volcanic mountains should be left to sturdy men who brave the perils and fatigues of the ascent in the interest of science and for the purpose of adding, by their observations, to the world's stock of knowledge."

24. The Mountain's Saint Bernards

In the Northwest, when someone is lost in mountains or forest, the call for help goes out to the Crag Rats. Like the city fire department or the U. S. Coast Guard, these men are equipped and ready with an emergency crew to go on rescue missions, and the rest of their comrades are pledged to follow whenever the advance guard sends back the call of necessity.

First aid equipment, ropes, crampons, a stretcher and food are ready for immediate transport to the scene of woe. In easy reach are mountain boots and sturdy garments to resist the cold storm blasts, skis and parkas for the winter trail. Like a fire alarm every call gets response at once, for that is the code of this volunteer group of men who live in the shadow — under the charm that Mount Hood imposes on all who seek communion with it.

Only men who have climbed Mount Hood and Mount Adams are eligible for membership and the Crag Rats, from the eligible host, invite their own comrades. No petitioner has ever been accepted. They must be physically fit for heavy work, must own skis, snowshoes and parkas, know first aid, be able to read maps, fight fire, know the country and be familiar with the fish and game laws of Oregon and Washington. To keep membership they must climb Mount Hood at least once a year.

At organization in 1926 they numbered 16; in 1937 there were only 33 members, but every one of them meets Crag Rats criteria. On rescue missions they spend their own funds. Without an accident they have escorted many hundreds of men, women and children to the summits of Mount Hood and Mount Adams as well as other peaks. Each year they stage their own particular "thrill climbs," visiting other mountains than their own two, and choosing the more difficult routes of ascent.

The Crag Rats, called by Stewart Holbrook, the writer, "the St. Bernards of North America," were organized August 3 1926 in the Hood River office of Andy Anderson. It succeeded another group, the Hood River Guides, who functioned as civic greeters, with none of the Crag Rats' qualifications for membership.

Among other points, the Crag Rats' articles of organization pledged all members to give aid in the mishaps associated with outdoor activities. Hardly had they signed their names when the first call came. No one then had heard of them; it was a general call for people who knew the mountains to help search for little Jack Strong in the Sandy River valley. They won instant fame when they found the lost boy at timberline in a few hours. Less than five months later the name won more luster when they rescued Calvin White as he lay near death in the snow above Government Camp.

Who were these Crag Rats? The query came from all sections of the country and the replies, published in magazines and newspapers of wide circulation, gave them national prominence.

In the following mid-summer Crag Rats were on Eliot Glacier for a ski tournament. The Mazama climb was proceeding up the Sunshine Trail at the time of the accident that resulted in the death of Dr. Stryker. The Crag Rats had taken a stretcher and first aid equipment to the glacier in case of accident; this they rushed to the scene and assisted with the victims. They improvised to meet the needs of the moment, even while the activity was obliged to dodge avalanches.

Their record since has won wide praise. A girl saved from a crevasse...stranded climbers brought down to safety...climber injured in fall on his ice ax saved by first aid work and carried out of danger. In addition they saved a man marooned on an island in the flooding Hood River, recovered the body of a man who fell into a crevasse in Ingraham Glacier on Mount Rainier, and took part in the search for two youths from The Dalles who perished on the Three Sisters peaks amid the Labor Day storm of 1927.

The Crag Rats filled a long felt need for an organized body

ready to move at once, with plans prepared in advance, for any kind of accident or loss in their area. The list of their deeds is long. In the first 11 years, members engaged in 20 rescue missions. When the strapping men uniformed with checkered blazers and mountain armlet reach the scene of trouble or disaster, they bring a feeling of confidence and hope.

For some years these men have been taking charge of a unique activity of war veterans, the annual Mount Hood climb of the American Legion, Hood River Post. Formation of the Crag Rats was inspired by these Legion climbs as its members were participating when Andy Anderson proposed the rescue group.

In 1921 with memories of the World War still fresh, members of the Coast Artillery Corps, Oregon National Guard, were making overnight hikes and they formed the nucleus of the Hood River Legion post. With Kent Shoemaker leading they climbed Mount Hood — with George Wilbur, Ned Van Horn, Robert Foust and Harold Hershner, he organized a program that included Ben Olcott, the Governor of Oregon, and Secretary of State Sam Kozer. With nearly 100 others they reached the summit.

Governor Olcott presided at the flag-raising on the summit, enjoyed a 200-foot slide on the way down, acquired a badly sunburned nose and pronounced the experience tremendous. He is the only governor to reach the mountain top while in office.

Since then the climb has been an annual affair, drawing Legionnaires from all parts of the country. For the first few years they camped at the head of Sand Canyon, and the climb involved a 3-mile hike from the old Hannum ranch, site of the present Homestead Inn, before timberline was reached. When the fine highway to Cloud Cap was completed, a spur road was built into the Tilly Jane campground, not far from where Mrs. David Cooper had officiated years before. On the south side of this place a camp has been provided for hundreds of visitors. All are fed army style and the low fee makes the outing possible for large numbers. In one climb a party of 270 made the summit.

Mark Weygandt guided these climbs for the Legion post until the Crag Rats took over. Each year they rotate the position of chief guide. Crag Rat members climb up the day before to break trail, clean loose rock out of the high chimneys and string the lifeline.

Then that route is closed by order of the Forest Service until the Legion party has gone up and returned. (This insures against avalanches started by other climbers.) The night before the climb sees the Crag Rats guarding the route.

Nearly 22 persons have been escorted to the top in the Legion climb without serious accident. In 1932 four persons suffered slight bruises when a small avalanche hit one of the roped parties on the descent, but Ed Goodrich, who was anchoring, saw the slide coming and braced himself to avert disaster.

The Sunshine Trail was developed after the Legion climbs began, and was followed in 1925 by one of Weygandt's large parties — on his 539th ascent. While the Sunshine route is considered the most spectacular on the mountain, it is longer and the Crag Rats feel it is easier and safer to control the big crowds on the straight and narrow road that lies along the Spur.

Sunshine Trail was so named because climbers are in direct sunlight practically all the way, up and down, and it avoids the treacherous icy slopes often found in the shadow of ridges. Weygandt developed it, and he made the first ascent that way with Andy Anderson and Donnerberg in June 1923. For the entire distance climbers are in the open, with spacious views all over. In addition to crossing two of the finest glaciers on the mountain, after attaining the arete they look down into Ladd, Sandy and Reid Glaciers and the Eden Park inter-glacier; they see distant glimpses of Zig Zag Glacier and the scenic Eden Park and Paradise Park, as well as the Wy'east Basin. Weygandt, in the latter years of his guiding, led most of his parties that way.

25. Stunt Climbers and the Stunters

Mountain climbers may be classified into two groups. The first consists of that greater number who ascend a peak for the thrill and to see the view from the summit.

The dyed-in-the-wool mountaineer has a number of reasons. He or she goes for the view, too, because from the top of a peak one sees new objects and enjoys different experiences each time. He also climbs for the love of the sport, for the exercise he gets and occasionally, if he is more venturesome, for the acrobatics. The field for the latter is large, even on Mount Hood, if the climber goes off the beaten trails for his effort.

Seeking out new routes is a quite recent development. After the main routes north and south had been explored, they were followed fairly closely for many years. Thousands trod up Cooper's Spur and past Crater Rock. When the mountain became more accessible because of improved roads, climbers began branching out.

The first trail, as noted before, was up the south side through the crater. The second was along Cathedral Ridge by Newton Clark in 1887. Soon after, climbers were being conducted from Cloud Cap across Newton Clark Glacier to the spur below Steel's Cliff, which was then ascended. Cooper's Spur route, the shortest and easiest on the mountain, and always popular with casual climbers, was next. Years later Mark Weygandt developed the Sunshine Trail.

Newton Clark's line up Cathedral Ridge has never been followed by large parties. The other four listed above have been the "commercial" routes because many of the climbers who passed over them were led by guides.

While the south side crater "boulevard" is considered the safest — and by some the easiest — it has been the scene of more serious accidents than any other route on the mountain. This in part is due to the greater number traversing it, but its very appearance of ease has caused some climbers to become reckless, and that is when the mountain takes its toll. Ice on the steep slopes and falling rock offer the chief dangers.

The snow chute above the Big Crevasse claimed a climber's life on July 5 1932 when three youths, climbing before the lifeline had been anchored, ran into ice in this sharp slope. They were unroped and equipped only with alpenstocks, and on the way down Glen Gullickson of Portland slipped and shot down the declivity to death on the rocks below.

The Wy'east Trail, a simplified version of the route followed by the Langilles up Steel's Cliff, has become increasingly popular as a spectacular climb over which parties may be conducted. Wy'east Trail was followed first in 1932 by James Mount and Everett Darr of the then new Wy'east Climbers group.

The rest of the routes are for the experts. Mount Hood does not offer the fine solid granite and sandstone slabs and aretes for the scaling that veteran rock climbers enjoy. Its lava formations are dangerously friable, and they fracture under slight pressure. The touch of a climber's hand often sends great masses crashing down. On any of the wall climbs of Mount Hood there is constant danger from falling rocks. The ice climbing is as good as any to be found, for Mount Hood's Glaciers present every kind of formation.

Everett Darr, the efficient chronicler of activities of the Wy'easters, has listed these additional approaches to the summit. In mounting order of difficulty, they are: A. up the west face, along but not over Yocum Ridge crest which remains unclimbed; B. the variations on Cathedral Ridge; C. the east face of Pulpit Rock; D. the headwall above Eliot Glacier on the northern expanse; E. the wall above the cirque of Sandy Glacier, also on the west side; and F. the direct assault on Steel's Cliff, inside the crater. Only in the last two years have all these places been conquered.

The Sandy cirque wall was ascended June 6 1937 by Joe

Leuthold and Russell McJury, both Wy'easters. They crossed the saddle above Illumination Rock, traversed Reid Glacier and Yocum Ridge and headed up Sandy Glacier. They then ascended the "rotten" rock of the disintegrating cliff, spending 4 hours of the 10 consumed in the entire climb to negotiate this treacherous face. Next to the crater wall ascent, this is considered the most difficult bit of mountaineering on the peak.

Gary Leach is a stunt climber of premier rank. He not only has set most of the records for speed, but has been in spots on the snowcap which no other human has touched. He went inside the crater wall directly across from Crater Rock, braving the almost continuous avalanching down this face, and using the most delicate of hand and footholds. Others have followed him since, but not until the mountain undergoes vast changes will any novice parties make it.

Leach also scaled the great crags one sees rising from the cliff near the top of the Eliot headwall. A fine view of their dizzy proportions is obtainable from the summit, under which they stand. The chief of these is known as Cathedral Spire.

Illumination Rock, on the southwest shoulder, is an isolated mass of abrupt proportions standing at the head of Reid Glacier's southern morainal wall. For many years considered impossible to climb, it was conquered by T. Raymond Conway. Its rock is the most stable on the mountain. Only because of its more resistant qualities has this wedge in the glaciers withstood the erosion that destroyed the rest of the wall of which it once was a part. For acrobatic climbers, it is considered the best rock feat in Oregon mountains. For a long time the only course was up its western face, but Leach, who traveled alone, made the traverse up one side and down another.

Pulpit Rock, on the north side, is the great nose of lava that projects down between Ladd and Coe Glaciers just before these two ice sheets merge. Pulpit is the upper pillar of the portal through which the glaciers join. Newton Clark led a climb in 1887 along the west side of Pulpit Rock, but the sheer east face defied all assaults until Irving Lincoln came along, another solo climber of high attainments, in 1936.

Cathedral Ridge, one of the longest buttresses of Mount

Hood, is a problem for mountaineers but it has been traversed several times. Sunshine Trail joins it high up, where the going is good, but the man who tackles the formation lower down must pass steep rock and avalanches. The first to make it were Mazamas George X. Riddell and H. H. Prouty in 1912. In one of the most notable ascents this way, Bob Osborn and Merle W. Manly started from the 1923 Mazama camp in Eden Park on what was intended as a reconnaissance, and wound up on top. En route they met two members of the Seattle Mountaineers who said they were "dropping down" the west side to visit the Mazamas. This pair swung to the right, however, along the complicated course and at nightfall found themselves staring over the sheer cliff at the tip end of Pulpit Rock. In sleeping bags on a precarious and uncomfortable perch they spent a night, before getting down to the west.

Only a few climbers have gone to the top of the wall above Eliot Glacier. After leaving the ice, a vertical distance over 3000 feet must be overcome — and much of it approaches the vertical. McJury and William Hackett made it in 1936, coming out directly underneath the lookout cabin. Those who have faced north from the summit to see the ice of Eliot Glacier far below yet almost underfoot, will appreciate the chances these youths took. Some years before, Mark Weygandt and Arthur Emmons also climbed the Eliot wall, but their route was farther west.

The Wy'east Climbers are a small group with a good record of conquest already larger than most mountaineering clubs. New climbs on the major peaks are their speciality, and they have had a part in most of these recent Mount Hood victories. The club was formed in December 1930 with Donald Burkhart as president, Ray Atkeson as secretary, and James Harlow, historian, with only four other charter members, Barrie James, Alfred A. Monner, Ralph Calkins and Norman O'Connor.

His comrades had the sad task of recovering Burkhart's body after he met death with Davis McCamant and John Thomas in an avalanche over the precipitous east slope of Mount Jefferson.

Wy'east members climb Mount Hood at all seasons, under all conditions. They are in the forefront of the annual dash for New Year's honors, and on one recent holiday, three of them, Calkins, Leuthold and Henry Kurtz stayed on Cooper's Spur all night in one of the winter's worst blizzards, in order to put their names first in the summit register.

The Wy'easters have to make at least three major climbs each year to keep in good standing. They took over the dilapidated old timberline cabin at Camp Blossom, but the increasing numbers of skiers crowded them out, so they built a sturdy cabin at the head of the first timberline road. It is often buried to the roof peak in snow but they flock there and make it a busy base for their strenuous enterprises.

All members are trained in first aid and, noting the numerous climbing accidents, they equipped a station at Crater Rock, with a toboggan, medical and surgical supplies, blankets and concentrated food. When the shelter hut at the head of White River Glacier was completed, this stuff was moved there. Soon it was being pilfered — blankets disappeared — splints available for fracture cases were used by irresponsible climbers to kindle fires. After thieves cleaned them out a couple of times the Wy'easters gave up this humanitarian endeavor.

In June 1937 Wy'easters Ralph Calkins and Henry Corbett, with Elsie Hall and Jean Blake, ascended the Sunshine Trail. Some 18 inches of snow had fallen just before the climb and dangerous avalanche conditions developed on the warm day. They were on their way down, just below the rock chimneys, when the snow began moving out underfoot. They were unable to anchor through to the firmer base beneath and soon they were shooting at tremendous speed down a 2000-foot declivity to where the mass broke over the wall. They fell 75 feet into the soft snow that had preceded them and piled up in a great heap. The two men suffered friction burns on hands and arms from the attempt to check their fall. Jean Blake was unscathed but Hall had to be carried off the glacier with painful injuries.

Ray Lewis was the summit lookout in 1933 when Mark Weygandt had his most harrowing experience with a climbing party. This occurred on that fateful weekend when Burkhart and his companions perished. Weygandt and his son Wesley were leading a group over the Sunshine Trail, crossing around the end of the big bergschrund at the head of Coe Glacier. Suddenly the roof of a blind crevasse collapsed and the rear end of the party started sliding in. Three had fallen below the surface when the rope sawed in two on the rough edge of ice at the lip of the crevasse.

Weygandt and his son found Mike Thomas, Eugene Mekley and Esther Gilman 25 feet down in the crevasse, on the broken ice of the bridge. The girl was disabled by injuries but the men were able to support her to where she could be hoisted to the surface.

The accident scene, a half-mile and 1000 feet in elevation below the summit, was clouded over and the biting cold wind was rising. The worst, crevasse-ridden part of the Sunshine route was behind them, so Weygandt decided to take the party on the shorter, safer climb to the top. With Mark leading, Wesley and Thomas carried the girl up the snow-covered arete. The wind was so strong that they were forced to stay below the crest to avoid being blown off.

Lewis had been watching this party most of the day. They disappeared under a shoulder and he became worried when they did not show again. Taking a rope and hot tea, he started down. He found the party struggling on the slope, fatigued, cold, battling strong wind and ice at more than 10,000 feet elevation, carrying the injured girl. Some in the party were near exhaustion and slipping. Frozen rain and snow drove horizontally in the gale.

Lewis hurried back up to the cabin and brought out 1500 feet of rope which, after great difficulty, he and the guides were able to lay down the ridge. They wrapped the girl in blankets and a canvas and tied the rope about her. She was dragged and carried the rest of the distance to the top. All this occurred after dark, amid driving fog and sleet, in freezing temperatures. They finally reached the lookout shelter at 10:30 pm.

Without complaint Gilman endured the ordeal. That night 13 men and women crowded into the 12-foot square cabin on top, while it creaked and swayed in the pounding gale. Next morning, as the storm went on, it was decided safer to take the girl down the south side. She was bundled up again, carried westward to the head of the chute, and tied in on the lifeline. Down she was slid and carried to the head of the hogsback, thence to Crater Rock. Lewis went to the cache where the Wy'easters kept their toboggan; with this the girl's traumatic journey was soon over.

26. Uncle Sam's Stewardship

Mount Hood is the property of the people. The line between Clackamas and Hood River counties lies across the peak itself, but title to its forests, glaciers, snowfields and ridges is vested in the federal government and dedicated perpetually to the public interest. At the southern base, a few hundred acres of homestead remain in private ownership, but the rest has been public domain, as now represented by the U. S. Forest Service, since this region was made a part of the United States.

Mountain areas from the first were destined to be federal lands, their utilities dedicated to the use of all the people. There was danger in the 19th Century that the better timbered sections might pass to private owners but this was checked after agitation by Will G. Steel and others. It resulted in creation by President Cleveland of the Cascade Range Forest Reserve on September 28 1893 — the beginning of forest administration. Already, on June 17 1892 President Harrison had set aside the Bull Run Timberland Reserve west of Mount Hood.

The Reserve was first administered in the General Land Office [*now Bureau of Land Management*], then transferred, in 1905, to the Forest Service as a bureau of the Department of Agriculture. Gifford Pinchot was the first National Forester.

In 1908 the Forest Service split up the old Reserve into the Oregon, Cascade, Umpqua, Crater and Deschutes forests. The Oregon Forest, renamed Mount Hood National Forest in 1924, originally had 1,787,000 acres, but was reduced when the Santiam watershed became part of the new Willamette National Forest. [*In 1990 it totaled 1.1 million acres.*]

The first men in charge of the Reserve included W. H. H. Dufur, Adolf Aschoff, D. B. Bronson and R. B. Wilson. Thomas H. Sherrard, who began service with the Reserve in July 1899, rose to supervisor of the Oregon Forest in 1908, and remained until 1933. He then stepped into regional supervision of recreational development, which, especially about Mount Hood, had become the most important feature of forest administration.

When Tom Sherrard became supervisor of the old Oregon Forest, he had plenty to do. Near Mount Hood were four permanent ranger districts, Zig Zag, Hood River, Wamic (now Dufur) and Estacada. In summer there were two more, Summit, at the south base of the mountain, and Clackamas Lake, astride the Cascade crest south almost to Mount Jefferson. On the south end were the Sisters, Detroit and Cascadia districts; with increased use, one more, Columbia Gorge Ranger District.

Many people believe the Forest Service exists chiefly for protection of forests, but this is only one activity. Timber cropping and sales, grazing of livestock, research for greater usage of timber products and forest perpetuation, and ranking with these in equal importance, recreation, which is now recognized as a major use of the national timberland resource. Policy aims to fit the lands for the use to which they are adapted for the greatest public benefit. It cannot be said that the Forest Service anticipated recreational development. It waited for public demand, then met it.

Thus the Forest Service did not build a road to timberline on Mount Hood anywhere until the need was shown. The first roads were made by other agencies. On the north these were private builders, on the south a rough wagon way by the U. S. Army for scientists establishing a timberline camp. Public demand can be said to have originated every improvement travel and shelter, sometimes long delayed, on the mountain.

The Mount Hood recreation area was dedicated in 1926 by the Secretary of Agriculture. The order said that national forest lands therein were "held for the use and enjoyment of the general public...coordinately with the purposes for which the Mount Hood National Forest was established. A proper and orderly use of the timber, forage, water power and other economic resources shall be allowed within the area, but the use shall not be permitted to impair the value of the area as a site for public camp grounds, municipal or health camps, sanitaria, club houses, hotels, summer homes or public utilities, requisite for the comfort and convenience of the people using the area for recreation purposes."

The Mount Hood Primitive Area, 14,800 acres, approved on February 13 1931, includes lands north and west of the mountain and part of the south, with the boundary extending northeast along Zig Zag canyon across the summit and down Cooper's Spur. Timberline Lodge and approach roads are outside the Area. Inside the Area no roads or occupancy permits are allowed; trails and public shelters are kept primitive. No grazing allowed, except by saddle horses and pack animals of visitors. Although not expressly prohibited, timber cutting will not be in the program.

Rough accomodations are provided in the Primitive Area. Backbone of transportation will be the Timberline Trail around the mountain, with spur trails connecting to places of unusual interest. Seven shelters — some of the "open-face" lean-to type — have been built on Mount Hood, at Crater Rock, Gnarl Ridge, Elk Meadows, Umbrella Falls and Camp Blossom, and two more in the Primitive Area at Eden Park and Paradise Park.

In the system also will be a new shelter building on the summit, replacing the cabin Coalman built. It probably will be ready in the summer of 1938, and will include a warming and rest room, storage space and lavatories.

Still alive is a permit for construction of a tramline and cableway from Cloud Cap Inn to the summit. It was granted to L. L. Tyler and associates after the issue had become the largest controversy ever to rage around Mount Hood. Application made in 1926 was for a cable railway to the top of Cooper's Spur and a suspended cableway from there to the summit, a distance of a mile. The proposal was made soon after Secretary of Agriculture Jardine set up the recreational area and raised the question of policy for future use and development.

Jardine, unsatisfied with what he heard from local committees favoring the permit, appointed another committee of leaders in various fields. They were Dr. John C. Merriam, president of the

Carnegie Institution of Washington; Frederick Law Olmsted, architect, and Professor Frank A. Waugh, of Amherst College. After much study of the region in 1929, the committee opposed the tramway, saying, "greater direct values from the area and greater fame for it could, in the long run, be secured without a tram and cableway to the summit than with it; …instead of aiming consistently at the very best results that can possibly be got out of the area as a whole, a beginning is now made, sacrificing some of these best values for the sake of an immediately popular detail, a precedent will have been set up for the gradual frittering away of extraordinary potentialities of the area."

One dissenting member of the committee warned that popular support for the tramway was great and denial of the permit might bring reaction against the Forest Service. That this could be true was shown in a meeting with the National Forester, W. B. Greeley, in Portland April 15 1927. Greeley spoke against the tram, but 15 of the most powerful groups in Portland and Hood River, as well as statewide groups favored it. Only three — the Mazamas, Trails Club and Oregon Technical Council — opposed.

Later, Arthur M. Hyde, who succeeded Jardine as Secretary of Agriculture, granted the permit. A document of interest, "Public Values of the Mount Hood Area," was issued in 1930 as a U. S. Senate publication by Senator Charles L. McNary. It covers the debate in much detail, together with the committee's report and a summary of data compiled by the Forest Service on the larger question of recreational values of the Mount Hood area.

The permit was offered if the sponsors could qualify — that is, raise enough money to assure the success of the project — but this they have as yet been unable to do.

Nor has the greater Cloud Cap project, which was sponsored a decade ago by a Portland group, been completed. This would replace the old lodge with a great hotel development. The Forest Service offered to build a highway if Portland and its Chamber of Commerce would sponsor a resort development and assure the government that it would succeed. The Forest Service then constructed the present "high gear" road connecting with the Mount Hood Loop highway, but the building proposal for the upper end never came off, chiefly because of the high cost involved.

There has been intermittent agitation to make Mount Hood a national park but thus far it has been successfully discouraged. Few desire it — least of all those who have sought the mountain year by year as a playground and retreat from the cares of life.

The tramline, the summit cabin and the Cloud Cap replacement were never built. World War II consumed the interest and resources of government. Cloud Cap owners worried that their lodge might not outlast the first winter's storms — 100 years later it still stands, cared for by the Crag Rats.

The Forest Service has undergone broad change in McNeil's "stewardship." The agency and its role have grown in size and complexity to serve a wide range of demands, some of them polar opposites. McNeil wrote of a less fractious world in the '30's. He was not concerned with big timber industry, as it had small place in the national forest before World War II. Now a large share of USFS time and resources go to this concern. And to the spotted owl, "timber management," protection against pests, and clear-cutting, among other controversies.

For basic indicators, this forest has 3783 miles of roads (300 miles paved) — advantageous to loggers and hikers — in seven ranger districts covering 1.1 million acres. While it dotes on building fish runs and the ecology for the spotted owl, the Forest Service spends even more effort on disposing of old growth trees.

One of its oldest responsibilities, on which Lije Coalman, Mark Weygandt and other pioneers labored, was fire protection. In almost 40 years, Mount Hood has experienced few major forest fires The presence of many more people in the woods — hikers, loggers, travelers, sportsmen — assures that fires are detected more readily than in past years.

Credit is due to better means of detecting and suppressing fires before they burn out of control, as well as more direct action to extinguish fires. Virtually all the lookout towers are gone, replaced by cruising helicopters and airplanes with infra-red instruments. They find the hot spots before fire and smoke develop. Special electronic devices locate lightning strikes (within a few feet) then relay such data on maps, by FAX machine, to firefighters in the field.

Fifty years after McNeil, we see technological advances in even more basics. "They had no power tools," said Jim Reick, who grew up in Zig Zag. "They did it all with hand tools— didn't have chain saws until '54 or '55." He has worked in the Mount Hood National Forest more than 30 years.

Multiple use involves much more — over 100 campgrounds and picnic sites, plus Cloud Cap Inn, Timberline Lodge, Multnomah Falls Lodge and the Barlow Road; six wildernesses totaling 186,000 acres, all with special rules for use; 1202 miles of hiking trails, including 111 miles on the Pacific Crest or "Skyline" Trail; five ski resort areas, mining exploration, and one Job Corps Center — not to mention the Columbia Gorge National Scenic Area, and miles of Scenic River protection on the Sandy and Salmon Rivers.

Growth caused the agency to set aside 165 miles of trail for skiing and other winter sports. In 1986, year-round recreation totaled 4.3 million visitor-days, viz., that many persons used facilities an average of 12 hours each.

One Forest Service source said it is "...more an arbitrator today. Can anyone balance all the multiple uses between Big Lumber, Big Environment and a wild mess of others from ski fans, artists, hikers and bikers and bear grass pickers, to horse lovers and wood cutters and snow bunnies?"

Whatever that answer, the multitudes come along with the roads and transport that entice them to this mountain. Mount Hood is the property of the people.

27. The Highway Girdle

As the Columbia River highway was the first long stretch of boulevard proportions to be built in the Northwest, so the Mount Hood Loop highway was the first standard constructed road to encircle closely one of the major mountains of the region. The Loop in fact is an arm of the scenic highway along the river, reaching out to enfold the mountain in the cluster of charms that for years made this road one of the most interesting on the globe. Great waterfalls, dashing torrents, the mighty River of the West, snowcaps and the lesser mountains, lava flows and fossil objects; the expansive orchards of the Hood River valley and the pleasant countryside of the south leg of the road are among the attractions of the Loop drive. Now has been added one of the greatest engineering feats of the era, the Bonneville Dam, harnessing the power of the river.

From the picturesque green hills of Portland, the traveler in a few score of miles rises to the base of the mountain and, at this high level, journeys two-thirds of the way around the peak. Here, the intimate views of the snowcap, because of the compactness and sheer rise of the tower from the glaciers and lava fields at its base, expresses size and power to far greater degree than loftier peaks of larger bulk, like Adams and Rainier. At its dedication the Mount Hood Loop was called the necklace about the old volcano with Portland as the pendant. Good simile — a necklace made up of gems, and the mountain, whose shoulders it covers, has been described as among the fairest on earth.

A creation of the federal, state and three county governments through which it runs, the Loop was opened June 21 1925. From Portland the entire circuit covers 173 miles. It reaches two summits, the highest, Bennett Pass, 4675 feet, which divides the watersheds of the Hood and White Rivers; the other, Barlow Pass, 4160 feet, on the main Cascade divide, separates the White and Salmon Rivers. At Barlow Pass it intersects Barlow road, over which the pioneers passed to the Willamette valley.

For about half of each normal year the highest part of the Loop (the portion from the Salmon River to the upper Hood River valley) is closed by heavy snows. Because of its importance as a primary highway connecting Portland with central Oregon, the southern leg is kept open continuously to the connection with the Wapinitia highway.

Like a mountain trail, this high section of the Loop has to be cleared of debris caused by the intense winter storms. Passing through the forests there is the annual attrition of the tempests among the shallow-rooted conifers. Mud and rock slides often come from the the melting snows on the steep slopes, and because of the drainage and unpredictable action of the forces in White River Glacier, the bridge over its alluvial fan is a wooden structure, replaceable quickly when carried away by the torrent.

For many years there has been agitation for an improved road to Mount Hood — even before the transition of horse-drawn to motor vehicles. E. Henry Wemme backed up his appeals by buying the Mount Hood and Barlow Road Company, removing the toll charge, and at his death the road was deeded to the state and became a part of the highway to the mountain. This was part of the stretch that Samuel Barlow opened after his memorable passage with the first wagon train in 1845 and 1846.

In the autumn of 1845, the Barlow party abandoned its wagons east of the summit and went on with incredible hardship to reach Oregon City. Barlow then obtained from the territorial legislature a charter for a toll road. In the following spring he hired 40 men to open passage to where the wagons had been left. This was accomplished in time for the immigration of 1846; that year 145 wagons, 1559 horses, mules and cattle, and one drove of sheep passed his toll gates. From 1848 to 1862 Barlow leased the road to various persons who did little but take toll. With little upkeep, the road became impassable. In 1864 the Cascade Road and Bridge Company took over, made improvements, built bridges and laid corduroy over the marshy places and on the long hills.

Ownership changed again in 1882 to the Mount Hood and Barlow Road Company, after the route lost much of its usefulness with completion of the railroad along the Columbia River. From this company Wemme bought the road.

Residents of Hood River valley had watched, perhaps with some envy, the stream of traffic moving into the Willamette country by Barlow Pass, and thought of a road of their own across the mountains to the west. Captain Henry Coe noted that the first attempt to build one began in June 1859 by Captain A. Walker. This was to run up the west fork of the Hood River, swing toward Lost Lake, then generally south over Lolo Pass (northwest of Mount Hood), the divide between the Hood and Sandy River watersheds. It would have intercepted Barlow's road near Sandy. With the shorter distance, Walker thought he could divert traffic from the Barlow road, but the enterprise was not completed, Only a few head of cattle passed through his gate.

Wemme's objective was a good road to Mount Hood and into the interior. The Loop apparently was not on his mind. About this time, about 1915, many in Hood River and Portland wanted a road across Lolo Pass, and the agitation was so widespread that the Forest Service made a survey and 3-1/2 miles of road were built. However, this would have cut into the Bull Run Water Reserve township that spreads over a large part of the upper Sandy basin. Portland city officials have zealously guarded the Reserve, hence the least suggestion of intrusion always has met a stiff fight. Water officials accused the Forest Service of running the survey for a railroad that would carry out logs to be cut at the edge of the Reserve. Opposition was so great that the Lolo Pass plan was abandoned.

Immediately followed the suggestion for a highway around the south and east sides of Mount Hood. It was an alternative for a public hungry to get closer to the mountain. Much credit for originating the Loop highway plan goes to Tom Sherrard. The U.S. Bureau of Public Roads sent T. Warren Allen to see if such a road was feasible. The first proposal was to begin at the end of the old Sand Canyon road, northeast of the peak, follow Cold Spring Creek to

Elk Meadow, thence through Hood River Meadow and Bennett Pass to White River, and follow the Barlow trail from there. This would have taken the highway somewhat higher and closer to the mountain than finally built.

Another suggestion was that the highway be carried rather high along Lookout Mountain, the ridge east of the east fork of the Hood River. The highway there would have provided almost continuous views of the mountain on the entire route. As built, close along the river, it follows low through forests and beside streams and waterfalls. Feasibility of the Lookout Mountain route has been demonstrated since in construction of a fire protection road there.

The Loop highway was a cooperative financial proposition. Governor James Withycomb signed the first application for federal aid, the first for any Oregon project.

James Schuyler made the location survey for the Bureau of Public Roads and with slight modifications he set the route. Construction began on the south side in 1919, starting from the Zig Zag Ranger Station to a point 2 miles beyond Government Camp. This included the difficult section up Zig Zag canyon and Laurel Hill. The following year crews went to work on the north end, in the Hood River Valley.

Construction took six years, and the route has been changed and improved many times since then. The major engineering difficulties probably were encountered at the White River crossing. This river meanders across the alluvial fan built up by the glacier, and often changes course. One month after the opening, the bridge collapsed and the highway was closed. In August a storm of winter intensity descended on the mountain, and drove the lookout from the summit. His telephone line was broken by sleet, and snow fell in Government Camp — in August. The abnormal precipitation swelled the flow of White River and it was soon in flood, undermining cliffs and cutting away banks. A great wall of mud, filled with boulders described "as large as houses," moved on the bridge and carried away most of it.

A stupendous exhibition of force was presented. The soft material of the meander plain was taken up quickly by the water to form a slurry which, for want of a better name, was called "liquid mud." This, not water, was what advanced down the glacial valley, and this mixture suffered no barrier to impede its progress. Estimates were of 100 tons a second passing the bridge. Higher up, great chunks of undermined moraine at the terminal of the glacier broke off and quickly were carried away. Large trees were wrenched loose and rode down, bobbing in the churning mass.

At the glacier's snout, miles above, spectators saw the terminal moraine disintegrating. Masses that had stayed put for centuries, as evidenced by the growth and death of trees on them, were dislodged.

In October 1930, following a deluge of warm rain which melted the autumnal snows at timberline, there was a similar occurrence. This time the bridge became a dam, boulders and other heavy debris carried by the stream lodging against it and tearing out bents. So great was the surge of the river that part of its waters cut a new channel and threatened to divert into the nearby Mineral Creek. Elsewhere, similar slides that looked like "sloppy cement," but composed chiefly of sand, flowed over the highway, bringing with them brush and trees, and buried the road many feet deep in places.

Glacial floods of this type have occurred here at least five times since this one, and signs at the bridge still warn of washout. You only need to see the yawning size of the White River upstream to appreciate the forces McNeil writes of.

Despite these tribulations, the Mount Hood Loop became at once a scenic route of great attraction. Further than the mere tour of the mountain, it is the axle of a series of radial spokes that reach into all sections of the region about. A network of roads has been spread since the Loop was built, and Mount Hood has seen its biggest development for the convenience of visitors.

The increased use of Mount Hood as a result of better accessibility brought about construction of the spur to timberline in 1930-31. It was first intended to accomodate climbers and hikers but it quickly became a popular route for all motorists. It was surveyed by Francis E. Williamson, the Forest Service recreation executive, and built at comparatively small expense. This road leaves the highway a short distance east of Government Camp and totals 5-1/2 miles length, with a public camp near the upper end.

Less than a half-mile east of this meadow stands Timberline Lodge, and extending back to the Loop highway from here is another road following the west fork of the Salmon River. The latter road, broader and not as steep, carried construction, and later the traffic of the many thousands of visitors to the Lodge. Then came a short stretch of road to connect these two, the old and new, and now there is a loop highway within the larger Loop. The west leg in 1937 was widened and "ironed out" to provide for heavy traffic.

Periodically since McNeil wrote, the state has rerouted, rebuilt, widened, upgraded, or otherwise changed the Loop. The continuous process reduced most of the adventures — doubtless some fun too — from this drive. It cut the total length around the circuit from Portland and return from 173 to 165 miles.

Eventually, too, the road was re-labeled in two sections — Oregon 35 between Hood River and the junction, just west of the Pioneer Woman's Grave, with U. S. Highway 26; from that modern interchange US26 runs southward through the Warm Springs Indian Reservation, and westward to Portland and the Coast.

Since 1937, traffic has multiplied in volume, with a steady run of trucks on US 26. Loop traffic year-around now averages over 5600 vehicles every day on US 26 and 1100 on OR 35, on yearly average, that is. Sadly, though, the accident record on this road has not much improved with time.

Change is most evident in three major ways. Construction of Freeway 84 made it a supremely easy, if not supremely beautiful, trip through the Columbia Gorge. The original scenic road (U. S. 30) remains open, in sections, for leisurely travel. With major improvements, Oregon 35 was opened in 1967 throughout the year, rather than closing in winter. Highway 26 has four traffic lanes over much of its length, and the notorious grades and twists on Laurel Hill have been tamed to a degree manageable by drivers of any skill level, though all must carry or use chains in winter season.

In the same way, the Timberline road has greatly improved. The original gravel road was a one-way loop not meant for private cars because of limited parking space at the Lodge. The present paved 6-mile two-lane road was built in 1956. Cross country skiers use the older Westleg road in winter; it is open to cars in summer. Lolo Pass road was opened for traffic in 1956, but snow and ice keep it closed in winter.

In more than a half-century, the famous Loop highway has lost little of its allure. In fact it is easier on drivers. As McNeil put it, the Loop "...is an arm of the scenic highway along the river, reaching out to enfold the mountain in the cluster of charms that for years made this road one of the most interesting on the globe."

28. The Winter Army Grows

Although many of us in the West like to say we live here because of long winters of cold and snow "back east," we do often cast a wistful eye at the Cascades when they wear the white of winter. The snow banks here are far deeper than anything seen in the hardest Eastern winters, but it's our advantage to take it or leave it. The snow is there. Go to it if you wish to hear its crisp crunching underfoot, or stay in mild clime and just admire the smooth whiteness from afar. You may regulate your dosage of winter sports almost to the minute — play golf in the morning, ski in the afternoon and have evening dinner far from the cold and snowfields.

The winter sports idea, despite mushroom-like growth in recent years, is neither fad nor new. From earliest settlement days the high Cascades have been visited in winter. Trappers were living snow-bound near timberline a century ago when settlement of the Oregon Country began. As roads made the region increasingly accessible, the winter traffic grew. Winter sports began surging after the highways were built and opened to all-winter use. With economical motor transportation available to almost everyone, the run from Portland to the south side recreational center can be made almost as fast as driving across the city. Many thousands enjoy winter sports each season.

The trip to Mount Hood is so common nowadays as to attract no stir, but it was a major undertaking in pioneer days. Skis were almost unknown; you prepared as if for an Arctic expedition; furs were a necessity; you went horse-drawn as far as you could up the old Barlow road, or by train to Hood River, then by stage up the valley to the horses' limit in deep snowdrifts. The rest of the journey would be made on snowshoes, with food supplies stored months in advance.

Preparations for such journeys received yards of publicity in the newspapers. Reporters met the heroes of the snowfields on return. It never seemed to occur to city residents that men and women were living year around, then as now in the "snow country" comfortably and safely, and finding the winter season as attractive as the warm months.

The Langilles and the other old-timers who lived at timberline in these months found that mild weather was the rule. The same warm winds from the ocean bathe valley and high elevations alike, and while snowfall might be deep, more often than not, in the brilliant sunshine the eaves of your cabin would be dripping and the fat pats of white on the branchlets of the firs would go slithering off as the warm rays softened them. But because of its inaccessibility, many believed it was a zone of Arctic cold.

Although Dick Maupin had been skiing about Summit Prairie for several years as a forest ranger, the first Mount Hood outing of the Mazamas in 1903 drew great attention. Sketches of the "hazards" they encountered went with the long account of the journey made that February by Colonel Hawkins, Martin W. Gorman and T. Brook White. With the announced intention of climbing as high as possible, they set out for Government Camp on what was called "a perilous trip." Their equipment included "plenty of furs to prevent being frozen to death."

Colonel Hawkins made skis 10 feet long, and each man had a 9-foot "balancing pole," used for turning as well as balance, suggesting a tight wire walker. They had snowshoes too. The "Norwegian skis" were described as "a good comparison to flying" by Hawkins, who said the trip was the pioneer winter outing of the Mazamas, "and I am sure we will now have our regular winter trips, which I consider are even ahead of summer outings." If this was portent of what was to be, read this by Brook White:

"While at Yocum's I prophesied that the time will soon come when more people will go to Mount Hood in winter than now go in summer, and I think my prophecy will soon come true. As soon as people find out what a delightful trip it is, all will want to go. The aspect of Mount Hood is infinitely finer than in summer."

It was a considerable chore to reach Government Camp in those days, much easier was the journey to Cloud Cap. Since the Inn was built, winter parties visited almost every season. J. Wesley Ladd of Portland was one of the leaders in early winter sports. Annually from 1901 to 1909 he led groups to the snowfields, usually on the north side.

Among these people sprang the idea of organizing, and so they formed the Portland Snowshoe Club. They were the first to use Norwegian-made skis on the mountain. Their clubhouse is a comfortable log structure on Ghost Ridge, a short distance north of Cloud Cap Inn. Construction began in July 1910 with Mark Weygandt as builder. He used logs from the forests below. Ladd, who was the first president, and Horace Mecklem chose the site. The other charter members were Harry and Elliot Corbett, David and Walter Honeyman, Rodney Glisan, Dr. Herbert Nichols, Brandt Wickersham, and Jordan V. Zan. Continuously since that time the clubhouse has been the scene of happy mid-winter parties.

The first group organized for skiing was the Portland Ski Club, formed in 1907. Members made an annual trip to Government Camp, usually in February.

Mazama winter sports trips became an annual event but the crowds were small and only the hardier members took part, as it involved long snowshoe climbs. A mountain lodge had been projected and winter sports activity was a chief factor in its location. The first lodge was built at Twin Bridges, below Laurel Hill, because even the most sagacious in the club could not foresee that an open road would be maintained that high. The Rhododendron vicinity had proved to be the normal winter limit for travel, so they purposely located the lodge some miles beyond. It was a comfortable snowshoeing and skiing distance so that the Mazamas' love for solitude would not be disturbed by too many visitors. The building scarcely had been dedicated when the highway department began the experiment of plowing snow, and the Mount Hood Loop highway was opened for winter traffic to Government Camp early in 1926. Cars loaded with snow-lovers followed close behind these plows. Winter sports for the multitude then began.

The Mazamas soon found their lodge was far below the skiing ground and they began planning another one higher up.

The best Mazama minds again chose a site far outside the mainstream of traffic, and built a fine lodge a half-mile east of Government Camp and 1000 feet above the highway. In the same year, the road went still higher and the first route to timberline nearly passed its door.

The Advertising Club of Portland sponsored development of a winter sports playground east of Government Camp, dedicated in 1927. The idea was to encourage recreation there and avoid mishaps such as the Brownlee-White tragedy. A toboggan slide was built, and a mild little ski-jumping hill, and provisions for sledding and skiing. Only in the last 10 years has skiing gone on in a large way at Mount Hood. Such a thing, though, as a comparatively small playground along the highway, never could hold skiers and they soon ranged many miles in every direction. They went but far above timberline. Skis have carried many climbers on a portion of the summit journey. Scarcely a foot of the mountain's southern slope nowadays misses the imprint of a ski track during the season.

Naturally, of course, the first ardent skiers would be of Scandinavian blood. Among them were experts from early years of training on terrain of northern Europe. Tournaments were staged. The first large ski hill was built on the east side of Multorpor Mountain, above the resort at Swim. Jumping tournaments began to attract crowds. The Mount Hood Ski Club was formed, then superseded by the Cascade Ski Club. The latter has spent thousands of dollars excavating its "master" hill and several smaller ones on the steep north slope of Multorpor. Three portable school houses were bought in Portland and combined for a clubhouse. Ski clubs of the Northwest joined up to form a division of the National Ski Association, and competitions were organized under regular schedules and rules governing world amateur sports.

The Portland Winter Sports Association was formed, a combination of business and civic groups to popularize winter sports. Later it became a statewide affair. The association's annual winter carnival and tournament has become an outstanding feature. While competition was first limited to jumping and racing, it has since expanded to include downhill and slalom races. The Ski Bowl on Tom, Dick & Harry Mountain proved to be the finest area in the West for the flag-gated slalom courses. The Cascade club's "big" hill has been the scene of competitions of national interest. The Forest Service built the Alpine ski trail from timberline to the highway.

The open slopes at timberline always have attracted the sturdier skiers and it is generally recognized that conditions there are superior because of the colder weather and consequent drier "powder snow." The handicap until recently was lack of adequate transportation. Nevertheless hundreds have gone there each weekend. Now, the excellent road to the new Timberline Lodge is being kept open all winter and this gives new impetus to winter sports.

All forecasts of the past about winter sports on Mount Hood have been short of what actually occurred. It would be reckless to estimate what it may attain in the future. With the Forest Service wholly alive to the importance of winter sports, developments are under way now that were undreamed a few years ago.

If the public response continues as quick as it has been in the past, the region is destined to become a winter sports center of ranking import with the greatest in Europe. The reason the Old World resorts are so widely popular lies in their accessibility — that and "good" snow. Mount Hood has the snow for a long season each year, and roads and facilities for public convenience are being steadily improved.

McNeil was an effective promoter, and though he wrote his forecasts in modest terms, he based them on his own activities and close identification with winter sports. He was one of the founding members and president of the Cascade Ski Club, the Pacific Northwest Ski Association and the National Ski Assn, and later elected to the National Ski Hall of Fame.

After World War II, at Government Camp he saw development of Multorpor, Ski Bowl and Summit Ski Area, and the increase of all kinds of winter sports. At the low end of the Eastleg Road, the old garage and base camp built for Timberline Lodge workers was converted to the Snow Bunny Lodge for sledding and other youth sports. On the north side was Cooper Spur Ski area.

Highway improvements and better-equipped cars McNeil could only guess about; the flood of traffic to and from the mountain every winter affirms his broad vision. A half-century after his day, his "winter army" continues growing.

Afterword

by Joe Stein

Lord of waterfalls, glaciers, high meadows,
of deep wilderness silence,
of frigid air and soughing skis,
Your mountains overwhelm us.
God of Joy, give us more than
five senses only.
This one time around we pray for the grace to live,
to love the life you gave us.

Fred McNeil called it "noble," a small word conveying images of a dazzling mountain. All at once he found it exhausting, inspiring, irresistible, near to Heaven. As did the white settlers. As do we ourselves.

In his book mountain magic lures everybody. And though it can turn barbarous in an instant, Mount Hood offers nothing to fear. Except for ignorance or carelessness those who answer its lure find only small risk.

What of savage beasts, snakes, poison oak, bugs or other nasties of the wild? They are rare, at most rarely encountered. Charles Lake, who knew McNeil while growing up in Rhododendron, learned a love of wildlife; he tends lame and injured animals at his home. He got his worst injury when kicked by a wounded deer; of dangers he said: "Nothing worse than mosquitos in season." Big animals and small, black bear, cougar, porcupine, bobcat, deer, elk, marmot, beaver, coyote, fox, raccoon, mole and the rest all inhabit the forest but avoid human contact. And a few snakes live in remote areas east of the peak. Lake avows that the animals have much more to fear from us than we from them.

In McNeil's stories danger arises from human weakness, dumb mistake or miscalculation. Clearly, the wild mountain is more gentle, more benign than a city park, and far more beautiful.

More than snow for skiers, stimulus for hikers and climbers, glaciers for explorers, and the challenge of forested highlands, this peak gives us pure air and water; it sustains the verdant land and challenges the human spirit. Sure, a mountain is itself among Earth's largest living things.

Volcanic fury was beyond McNeil's ken when he wrote, "Far from an occasion for alarm...an eruption would provide one of Nature's most sublime spectacles." Common belief in 1937.

For over a century, residents of a land studded with volcanos had meager experience with eruption, vague ideas of what an exploding mountain might do, plus a generous dose of hearsay. They knew of occasional rumbles, over-blown tales of fire and smoke from craters, a bit about 1914-16 blasts of Lassen Peak in California. They hardly understood the geologists, who learned by tedious study and exploration of the mighty Cascades.

Forty-three years after McNeil wrote, Mount St. Helens stirred awake. The snow peak on Washington's southwest horizon shook and rumbled for three nervous months. Then, without warning, on May 18 1980, an eruption blasted more than a cubic mile off the peak — with a roar heard or felt over a large part of earth.

For much of a day the volcano spewed superheated rock, steam and ash as high as 15 miles in the sky, and clogged the rivers with mudflows. It crunched the 9677-foot peak down to a cratered ruin with an 8300 ft. top, and affected the global climate for months. A decade later, dredges continue to clear mudflow from nearby rivers, and the influence of that eruption persists. The blast killed 60 persons and injured many hundreds — so far as known — destroyed 235 square miles of prime forest, and devastated a great expanse of land along the Toutle and Cowlitz river valleys all the way to the Columbia river.

The Northern Pacific Railroad owned St. Helens from a 1917 federal land grant. If the title holders pondered what it means to *own* a volcano we have no record....nor whether such ownership might be like managing tidal waves or thunderstorms. The railway deeded it over to the national forest in 1980, and it now has national monument status.

Who owns Mount Hood, 60 miles southeast of St. Helens? We who live around Zig Zag (this writer included) took avid interest in St. Helens's outbreaks. Our snowcapped peak looked as solid as — well, as a mountain — even while geologists cited the colossal forces under our feet. Our homes rest on the efflux from four documented major eruptions of Mount Hood in 10,000 years.

Do these two mountains answer to the same Monster? Dare we ignore the fumaroles and the quakes we feel from time to time? *Can it happen here?*

Yes it will happen some day. We can question human audacity with such risk. On July 11 1980, weeks after the St. Helens cataclysm, U. S. Geological Survey in Washington D.C. issued a news release about a Mount Hood "quake swarm" that "spurred a special monitoring effort" on Mount Hood. As if treading our nerve ends, it said, "Scientists noted that the eruption of Mount St. Helens was preceded by an unusual number of earthquakes...." And composite volcanos follow a common pattern of behavior.

Does this mean imminent eruption of Mount Hood? Well, no. Local experts derided Washington's "news." They linked some of those tremors to forest work — blasting stumps on the mountain. Over many decades they have regularly tabbed quakes and shakes.

Dr. John Eliot Allen, noted geologist and author, sees "No cause to worry about it. With what we know now, we will give ample warning to residents — several weeks at least — before a major event. The Survey constantly monitors instruments at strategic places on the peak."

Such earthquakes and harmonic tremors, Allen asserted, offer a fine way to study vulcanism. Earth science got "very valuable information" through study of St. Helens before and after the eruption. History's best opportunity to observe a composite volcano in action. The geologists' warnings helped cut the loss of life on St. Helens. They gave the authorities time to evacuate the residents and otherwise prepare for the worst.

Dr. Allen still calls Mount Hood "dangerous," capable of large ash falls and pyroclastic flows, which come on like firestorm. Worse, he said the amount of glacial ice present on the peak — some three times that of St. Helens — could melt and overpower the Sandy, Zig Zag, White and Hood rivers with mudflows. This could work havoc on mountain villages and the fast growing cities as far as east side Portland. In spite of timely warning, "by experience we know some people won't listen....And, many times more people live near Mount Hood than did at St. Helens."

Mount Hood's latest eruption, about 1790–1810, gushed great mudflows into the White, Sandy and Zig Zag rivers, and dumped ash on a wide area. There was evidence in the 1805–06 journals of Lewis and Clark, whose exploring party crossed the "Quicksand" (Sandy) river, then clogged by mudflow, where it joins the Columbia. Minor eruptions occurred in 1859–65.

Geologists insist Mount Hood will blow "soon." They talk aeons and epochs, yesterdays and tomorrows measure in centuries. Meanwhile, living the good life here, we understand people who dwell elsewhere with the risk of tsunami, flood, tornado and hurricane, parched desert and storm-racked seashore, or the earthquake zones of Armenia, Japan and Algeria. We note that the USGS itself has an office at Menlo Park, astride the tremorous San Andreas Fault of California, 30 miles from San Francisco.

So we romanticize Harry R. Truman, the aged man who refused to leave his lodge on Spirit Lake, now buried under 200 feet of rubble from St. Helens. Our own mountain has historic shrines — Cloud Cap and Timberline Lodge — up there in the likely path of eruption. In the tradition of McNeil's pioneers, Truman was not afraid of the worst, not afraid of life. Or death.

We may savor McNeil's words on the "sublime spectacle." He wrote that with newsman's instincts and, as well, the fervor of the witness on scene. Knowing it by climb and hike, by snow-shoe and alpenstock and ski, by horse and auto, he lived it for over 45 years — all his life after he arrived at age 19.

McNeil the newsman took an avid part in rescues but never put his own name in his narrative. We know he would be keenly interested to see the past half-century of development in the rescue system, improvements in finding and aiding the lost, the injured and wayward. It has benefits from technology — search equipment and methods, communication and medical aid, all far better and more reliable now than in his day.

Without doubt, medical science would impress him, advances in treatment for hypothermia, broken bones and internal injuries. Derived partly from the Viet Nam battlefront, it has intensified the fight against *trauma*. The unique speed and agility of the helicopter serves to rush treatment direct to almost any accident scene, then place the victim in best of hospital care in a matter of minutes. Trauma, a deadly one-hour clock, demands instant intervention before *shock* sets in.

Rescue is aided, more so, by ingenious sensing equipment and radio gear to deal with the worst of weather. For example, the rescue people can use a portable FAX machine to send maps and other such data into the wild. It is the same with planning and training, and with clothing and motorized rescue vehicles.

McNeil's stories too often begin on a grim note — the alarm sounded long after somebody was injured or missing. That too has improved, as mountain climbers and skiers know the basic rules of preparation. They know more about sudden storms and other risks. Winter resorts have electronic beepers available; these make it easier to find you if you do not return on schedule. And the wise explorers register with a resort, or the Forest Service, so that a search can begin right away if needed.

Still, there are exceptions. Even McNeil wrote about the errors of the careless and the unknowing who got lost up there. Mount Hood was to witness one more of its many tragedies on a spring day in 1986 — a May climbing party of 13 from the Oregon Episcopal School in Portland. With the four boys and six girls were two leaders and an experienced guide.

Near the top, a ferocious blizzard struck. In the whiteout

they took shelter in a snow cave at the 8300-foot level. Next morning the guide and a student braved the continuing storm and frigid wind, and found their way to summon help. Bad weather stymied the best efforts of a massive search, and the rest of the party was not found for two more days.

Three climbers had left the cave. Rescuers found their bodies, encased in ice, and located the other eight, finally, under deep snow. Although rushed to hospital by helicopter, six died. Two survived the ordeal despite body temperatures barely over 70 degrees. Brinton Clark, 15, and Giles Thompson, 16, owe their lives to heroic rescue work and fast transport into hospital, plus advanced treatment for extreme hypothermia. Thus ended Mount Hood's worst climbing accident for loss of life.

A 1973 law mandates all Oregon counties are to devise rescue plans and take responsibility for searches. The state reserves a radio frequency exclusively for rescue service. The sheriffs of Hood River and Clackamas counties have such plans in place for Mount Hood.

They rely heavily on the kind of high calibre, hardy people McNeil knew in his time, but today they use more scientific means and methods in searches. For example, they have data guides to profile lost climbers and provide clues for the search team. They train together with all groups and agencies involved.

"Rescue people," said Neil James, Clackamas County Sheriff Lieutenant, "haven't changed in a hundred years. They have the savvy and stamina, and you can rely on them." While regretting the Episcopal School tragedy, he pointed to the great difficulty of dealing with the weather in that incident, and noted that two lives were saved.

The mistakes made differed little from those of Brownlee, Van Norman and Frederic Kirn, the others of McNeil's history. Every year more people visit the mountain. The Clackamas sheriff, who guards 1879 square miles of urban, farm and forest land, plus lakes and rivers, conducted 75 searches — 26 on Mount Hood — in 1989; in the smaller Hood River County, Sheriff Kelly did 10 searches. This promises more hectic rescue work in the future.

Timberline Lodge was completed just as McNeil's book went

to press and President Franklin D. Roosevelt dedicated it September 28 1937, the same day he did honors for the Bonneville Dam. He rode in a car owned by McNeil's friend, Horace Mecklem.

The President seemed to sense that the Lodge answered great popular demand. For many years that area of the mountain was the jumping-off place, winter and summer, for thousands of ski fans, hikers and climbers. McNeil often wrote of "timberline."

The Lodge project began with a modest sum, even for those days, of $275,513. It involved hundreds of workers, plus a troop of Civilian Conservation Corps youths who built one-way, gravel access roads. Because of scarce parking space, visitors at first rode buses between the Lodge and Government Camp.

After a long series of surveys and discussions, the Lodge was placed with care to fit its surroundings within easy access to existing roads. McNeil saw a vision: "...its broad lines and the long encircling wings suggest strength and security and warmth. It seems hardly possible that a more effective union of man-made structure to its natural surroundings could be conceived."

Emmett U. Blanchfield, then a USFS landscape architect, has detailed the endless pains and planning taken to find the exact site. They included work on a small pond down below, within commanding view to the south, to create elegant Trillium Lake.

Carried out as a WPA relief project of the Great Depression, the Lodge created jobs. The skilled and unskilled cut and hewed great timbers, shaped stone and iron, wove cloth and tapestries, carved wood and made paintings, to fashion a notable piece of architecture. Nearly $1 million was spent, finally, on the project. At a time of high unemployment when millions strove for daily bread, some saw it as a luxury for the rich. But it was a livelihood for artists and craftsmen as well as laborers.

Right away the new facility attracted skiers and climbers. What they found was a work of art on a grand scale — a treasure fashioned by Oregon people on a mountainside; it is today a National Historic Landmark.

Near Lodge completion time McNeil wrote, "Highways and trails have opened [*mountain recreation centers*] to the easy access of thousands. Some of the old timers see these changes with regret. They would keep the peak for those who have the strength and courage to face the difficulties attending its approach. But Mount Hood has room for all, the weak with the strong, and there are plenty of places about the peak which will be attained, as before, only by those who take the risks to get there.

"The glaciers will still have crevasses, the cliffs release their daily avalanches, storms will drape their impenetrable curtains, ice will glaze the snow; the going, above timberline at least, will remain as rough as it was for those who made the first climbs....the adventurer will have to slog along his own way as always, with a wary eye cast upward at the besetting elements of land and sky which no benevolent government as yet has been able to regulate."

Timberline Lodge opened for business on February 5 1938. By then the clouds of impending world war captured the Nation's main interest and resources. That posed a continuing challenge for the Forest Service. It lost money and stood empty for years before it became a viable enterprise.

Hard times for Lodge operators brought a succession of men or groups to manage it. It made its first profit in 1948 and that was meager. It deteriorated from heavy ski traffic and low maintenance. It closed November 30 1942 for three years of war, and was shut down once more on February 17 1955.

On June 1 1955 Richard L. Kohnstamm, a social worker from New York City, came to stay. As he told it 34 years later, "I caught the wave of the ski boom, but it was never easy. It took 30 years to do what I thought would take 10. The former managers mostly tried to run it from Portland....I knew that a hotel this large could not succeed with only 59 rooms."

Liquor by the drink — new to Oregon in 1953 — helped, said Kohnstamm. This tireless man of all tasks said he "did every job there is on this mountain. At first we dug cars out of the snow by hand, then the wind would drift it back. One night, just after we cleared it, another 4-foot snowfall dumped on the parking lot. On the slopes the snow was mostly cottage cheese. We had to process it for good ski surface.

"The skiers really saved it; they paid the expenses."

Another factor led to Kohnstamm's success, a willingness to deal with unpredictable climate. "The Indians never trusted it, with good reason. One day will be absolutely gorgeous, the next is filled with atrocious storms — without warning."

Paved roads, now open throughout the year, a large parking lot, heated outdoor swimming pool, ski lifts up to 8600 feet, a convention center, a Day Lodge for winter and summer sports, the Silcox Hut shelter up the mountain — all these have been added to make Timberline one of the most notable attractions on the Pacific Crest. And Kohnstamm dreams of adding more.

As a work of art indigenous to one of the world's most beautiful mountains, the Lodge has lured millions. Many writers have extolled it, notably in the 50th anniversary book, *Timberline Lodge, A Love Story.*

Like Timberline, Mount Hood Meadows was created in response to pressure from the winter sports fans, especially those who wanted to ski the drier, lighter snow on the mountain's east flanks. Other pressures came from the north side, seeking better access to ski slopes.

Because the Loop was closed on the east side in winter, from Cooper Spur Junction to the Highway 26 junction, that large area was inaccessible to skiers. From the Hood River Valley it was a drive far out of the way — 100 miles and more, around the west side of the mountain — to reach the south side resorts.

In 1966, the state agreed to open the road and keep it free of snow. A Portland consortium built the Meadows resort. It opened in December 1967. Hood River Valley partisans were somewhat mollified when the name Hood River Meadows was changed to Mount Hood Meadows, as more suitable to the location.

The Meadows grew fast to its present large size, with nine chairlifts, elaborate day lodges, lounges and shops. It is open only in winter. (It serves windsurfers at a branch in Hood River, in summer season.) Its owners have plans to expand for year-round use — subject to Forest Service approval.

In 1989 Government Camp stirred itself from the long decline that had begun with World War II. With county aid the town has made elaborate plans for "urban renewal" and expanded services. A proposed tramline lift to Timberline Lodge will replace the hazard of 6 miles of deep snow on Timberline Road.

The course of growth never ends. Windsurfers from over the world discovered the constant strong breezes at Hood River, and, in 1987, Congress created the Columbia Gorge National Scenic Area on Mount Hood's north flank. This will help to preserve the wonderland for posterity. And more millions of visitors.

More and larger resorts, more tourists, more traffic on the roads and the snows and the trails and in the forest havens — these and other abundant signs verify the lure of mountain that beguiled the early settlers and an endless line of followers, including one young Fred McNeil from Illinois.

We mountain dwellers understand what stole his heart.

VISITORS GUIDE

Whether you go by bike or hike or horsepower, it's a long way around Mount Hood. A long way to the top, too, in any season. Mountain roads and trails grow apace as the years pass, and they draw more people. Certain residents prefer fewer roads and visitors, but that view belies the open-hearted welcome of the Northwest highlands.

To the 1.1 million-acre Mount Hood National Forest add a few hundred thousand acres in private hands or held by federal, state and local governments. Altogether, a green-and-white wonderland of hills, blue lakes and tumbling rivers. At lofty elevations the winter snows pile up while the thermometer dives low. An added grand feature is the picture-card Columbia River, where ever-blowing breezes provide a world center for windsurfers, now officially the "Columbia River Gorge National Scenic Area."

The campgrounds, ski areas, hiking and climbing trails abound in this land, plus the only summer ski place in USA. Lodging convenient to the resorts is sparse, and public transit, thin. Distance between Hood River and Portland — 65 miles; Portland and Government Camp — 60 miles; Hood River and Mount Hood Meadows — 33 miles; between Meadows and Government Camp — 9 miles; between Portland and Zig Zag, at the west edge of the Mount Hood National Forest — 40 miles.

A car is essential here, but Oregon's roads are generally very good. Drivers must carry or use tire chains for winter's hazards, and your "SNO-PARK" pass ($9.50 for season) finances an efficient sanding and snow removal system. Government Camp and the ski centers are situated at 3500-ft. level or higher. Facilities in Hood River Valley and west of the mountain — all below 2000 ft. — usually have little or no snow. The mild climate, even in winter's grip, often surprises newcomers.

The following list samples the places and resources of interest to visitors. Reservations always advised. *Except as shown, all are Oregon addresses, with telephones in Area Code 503.*

Information, Reservations, Transportation

COLUMBIA GORGE NATL. SCENIC AREA, information, Hood River (386.2333).

GORGE CENTRAL SERVICE, Hood River, windsurfing, reservations, (386.5787, 386.6109, FAX 7560).

HOODLAND CHAMBER OF COMMERCE, Box 819, Welches 97067 (622.3017).

HOOD RIVER CHAMBER OF COMMERCE, Marina Park, (386.2000).

HOOD RIVER TAXI, 315 Oak St. (386,2355).

MOUNT HOOD RECREATION ASSN. RV-Village, Brightwood (622.3162, 622.3017).

MOUNT HOOD EXPRESS, Box 559, Welches 97067, van transport service (622.5554, Portland 250.4379).

PORT OF HOOD RIVER, Marina Park, Box 239, Hood River (386.1645).

SANDY AREA CHAMBER OF COMMERCE, Box 536, Sandy 97055 (668.8284).

MOUNT HOOD NATL. FOREST, Service Centers — information, books, maps:

Supervisor, 2955 NW Division St. Gresham 97030 (666.0700).

Zig Zag Ranger District, Hwy 26, Zig Zag 97049 (622.3191)

Hood River Ranger Dist., Hwy 35, Mt.Hood-Parkdale 97041 (352.6002).

Barlow Ranger Dist., Box 67, Dufur 97021 (467.2291).
Columbia Gorge Ranger Dist., 31520 Woodward Rd.,Troutdale
97060 (695.2276).

WILDWOOD RECREATION SITE, BLM, Hwy 26, 4 mi W Zig Zag
(622.3696).

Major Resorts

COOPER SPUR SKI AREA, Box 977, Hood River 97031, on Cloud Cap
Rd., 25 mi. S Hood River, 4 mi. off Hwy 35, at 4000 ft. level =
400 ft. vertical, T-bar, rope tow, race stadium; beginners &
intermediate, day lodge, rentals — Winter Season (352.7803).

LOST LAKE, USFS Hood River Dist., 30 mi. SW Hood River, summer
only, fishing, campground, hiking, picnics, no boating
(352.6002).

MOUNT HOOD MEADOWS, Box 470 Mt. Hood OR 97041-0470, 33
mi. S Hood River on Hwy 35, 65 mi. E Portland via Hwy 26 =
2873 ft. vertical, 9 chairlifts, complete sports shop & rentals,
lounges, 2 day lodges, 4 restaurants, Winter Season (337.2222;
Portland 246.7547).

MOUNT HOOD R V VILLAGE, 65000 Hwy 26, 4 mi W Zig Zag, 214-
acre forest land on Salmon river, 550 RV spaces; hiking, covered
swimming pool, sauna, spa, Year-Round (622.4011).

RIPPLING RIVER RESORT, 68010 Fairway Av., Welches 97067, deluxe
guest rooms and condos, 27-hole golf course, tennis, sport shop,
equipment rentals, convention facilities, coffee shop and dining
room, outdoor heated swimming pool (622.3101).

SKI BOWL, Box 280, Hwy 26, Government Camp 97028, on
Multorpor Mountain = 1500 ft.vertical; 4 chairlifts, surface tows,
helicopter; shops, rentals, 4 day lodges, Winter Season, Alpine
Slide in summer, (272.3206 or Portland 222.4158).

SUMMIT SKI AREA, Box 385, Government Camp 97028 = 400 ft.
vertical, rope tow, double chair; beginner & intermed., sliding
hill, rentals Winter Season (272.3351).

TIMBERLINE LODGE OR 97028, 65 mi. E Portland, at 6000 elevation = 1500–2500 ft. vertical,year-round & night skiing, 5 chairlifts, ski school rentals, Day Lodge for all mountain sports; 59 rustic guest rooms, lounges, shops, snack bar and dining room, outdoor heated pool, spa and sauna, (272.3311; 622.4072 — 800.452.1335, Portland 231.7979).

Where To Go

CASCADE LOCKS HIST. MUSEUM, Cascade Locks (374.8535).

COLUMBIA ART GALLERY, 207 2d St., Hood River (386.4512).

COLUMBIA TREKS & TRAILS, Odell, guide svc. (354.1574). ENNA POTTERY, 20600 Lolo Pass Rd., Zig Zag, ceramic studio (622.4546).

EXECUTIVE RIVER ADVENTURES, Welches, rafting (622.3153)

FALCON WHITEWATER, 4495 Riordan Hill, Hood Riv., guide svc. (386.2175).

THE FRAME ART GALLERY, 110 4th St., Hood River (386.1844).

FLY FISHING SHOP, Hwy 26 Welches shop. center, guided tours (622.4607).

HOOD RIVER AIRPORT, Airport Dr., Hood River (386.1732).

HOOD RIVER COUNTRY CLUB, 1850 Country Club Rd, 9-hole golf (386.3009).

HOOD RIVER DISTILLERS, Port Site (386.1588).

HOOD RIVER MUSEUM, Marina Park, historical (386.6772).

HOOD RIVER SPORTS CLUB, 3230 Brookside Dr., fitness (386.3230).

HOOD RIVER VINEYARDS, 4693 Westwood Dr. (386.3772).

HUNTERS' EXPEDITIONS, rafting, (389.8370)

HUSUM HILLS, Hwy 141, White Salmon WA, 18-hole golf (509.493.1211).

MOUNTAIN SPORTS RENTALS, Hwy 26 Welches shopping center (622.4737).

MOUNT HOOD RAILROAD, 110 R R Av. Hood River, scenic rides (386.3556).

MULTNOMAH FALLS, I84 Fwy = Second highest falls in USA, hiking, cafe, gift shop (666.4938).

MULTORPOR STABLE, Government Camp 97028, group rides (272.0228).

NORTHWEST SCHOOL OF SURVIVAL, Sandy, mountain climbing (668.8264).

PETER BYRNE EXPEDITIONS, Parkdale, guide service (352.7392).

PHIL'S GUIDE SERVICE, Rt 1 Box 552, White Salmon WA (509.493.2641).

RAINBOW TROUT FARM, 52560 Sylvan Dr., Sandy 97055 (6232.5223).

SNOW BUNNY LODGE, Government Camp, sledding, Winter Season (272.9205).

THE BOOK PLACE, Welches, books, gifts (622.3280).

THE DALLES AIRPORT, Dallesport WA (767.1114).

THREE RIVERS WINERY, 275 Country Club Rd., Hood River (386.5453).

TROUT & TREE, Mt. Hood-Parkdale, fish farm (352.6090).

ULTIMATE RIVER EXPERIENCE, Brightwood, guide svc. (622.3153, 666.6223).

WAUCOMA BOOKSTORE, 212 Oak St., Hood River, books, ceramics (386.5353).

WHITE CAP BREW PUB, brewery, 506 Columbia St. Hood River (386.2247).

WY'EAST EXPEDITIONS, guide service, Mt. Hood-Parkdale (352.6457)

FOOD AND LODGINGS This list samples the accomodations and eating houses North, South and West of Mount Hood, along the Columbia River, and in the Hood River Valley.

South and West

Restaurants

ALPINE HUT & LOUNGE, Hwy 26, Rhododendron, cafe 7 days, (622.4618).

BARLOW TRAIL INN & LOUNGE, Hwy 26, Zig Zag, 7 days, cafe, takeout, Western music weekends (622.3877). CHALET SWISS, Hwy 26, Welches, dinner, Wed–Sun. (622.3600).

CHARLEY'S MOUNTAIN VIEW, Government Camp, tavern (272.3333).

DARR'S MOUNTAIN SHOP, Government Camp, 7 days, (Wed–Sun winter), cafe, ski shop, rentals (272.3255).

DON GUIDO'S ITALIAN CUISINE, Hwy 26 Wemme, dinner 7 days (622.9977).

HUCKLEBERRY INN, Government Camp 97028, 7-days, tavern, cafe, ski shop, cross-country & downhill rentals (272.3325).

INN BETWEEN STEAK HOUSE, Hwy 26 Welches, tavern, 7 days (622.5400).

IVY BEAR, HWY 26, 9 mi W Zig Zag, European dinner 6 nights (622.3440).

LOG LODGE REST. & LOUNGE, Hwy 26 Rhododendron, Wed–Sun, Chinese & Amer., takeout (622.4865).

LOS AMIGOS, Hwy 26, 13 miles W Zig Zag, Mexican dinner, Wed–Sun, no-smoking, (668.5444).

MICHAEL'S MOUNT HOOD DELI, Hwy 26 Welches, Tues–Sun, cafe, home-made bread and pastries, takeout (622.5222).

PIONEER CAFE, Welches Rd at Hwy 26, seasonal hours (622.5333).

SALAZARS AT ZIG ZAG, Hwy 26, dinner only (622.3775).

ZIG ZAG INN & LOUNGE, Hwy 26, Zig Zag, Pizza, American Italian, 7 days (622.4779).

Lodgings

ENGLAND'S LODGINGS, Box 9, Government Camp 97028, cabins, chalets, apts. for 80 persons (272.3350).

FALCON'S CREST, Box 185, Government Camp 97028, bed & bfst. adjacent Ski Bowl (272.3403).

MOUNTAIN SHADOWS, Box 147, Welches 97067, bed & bfst. secluded in forest near Zig Zag (622.4746).

OLD WELCHES INN, 26401 Welches Rd, Welches, 1890 historic hotel, (622.3754).

OREGON ARK MOTEL, 61700 Highway 26, Brightwood 97011 (622.3121).

SHAMROCK MOTEL, 59550 Hwy 26, Brightwood, 20 units (622.4911).

SNOWLINE MOTEL, Highway 26, Rhododendron 97049, 9 mi w Ski Bowl (622.3137).

THUNDERHEAD LODGE CONDOMINIUMS, Box 129, Government Camp 97028 (272.3492).

TROLLHAUGEN, Government Camp 97028, room for 30 under one roof, ski shop, (272.3223).

VALU-INN MOTEL, Government Camp 97028 (800.443.7777).

WHISPERING WOODS CONDOMINIUMS, 444 Woodruff Way, Welches (622.3171).

North Side, Columbia Gorge

Restaurants

CASCADE INN, Cascade Locks, cafe, 7 days (374.8340).

THE CLUBHOUSE, 1850 Country Club Rd., Hood River, cafe, 7 days, (386.5022).

THE COFFEE SPOT, 12 Oak St., Hood River, 7 days (386.1772).

EDNA'S COUNTRY KITCHEN, Parkdale, country cooking (352,6540).

HOOD VIEW DELI, Hwy 35, Mt. Hood-Parkdale, seasonal hrs. (352.6202).

KAMPAI, 113 3d St., Hood River, Japanese, lunch & dinner (386.2230).

MESQUITERY, 1219 12th St., Hood River, grill & tavern (386.2002).

OLIVIA'S, Oak St., Hood River, Mexican cafe (386.3305).

MID-VALLEY IGA, 3380 Odell Hwy, Odell 97044, cafe & deli (354.2599).

ROSAUER'S, 1867 12th St. HOod River, deli 7 days (386.1119).

STONEHEDGE INN, 3405 Cascade, Hood Riv. restaurant, Wed–Sun (386.3940).

WEATHER RAIL, Marina Park, Hood River, lunch & dinner (386.3997).

WESTSIDE RESTAURANT, 1911 Cascade, Hood River, Ital., 7days (386.5747).

WYEAST NATURAL FOODS,5t & Oak Sts., Hood River, week days (386.2876).

YAYA'S INTERNATIONAL CAFE, 207 Oak St. Hood River, Greek (386.1996).

Lodgings

COLUMBIA GORGE HOTEL, 4000 Westcliff Dr., Hood River, 1920 Natl. Historic Site, on Columbia river overlook, 46 units, conventions (386.5566 or 800.826.4027).

COLUMBIA RIVER GORGE RESORT, Carroll Rd. Mosier 97040, 15 unit motel, 500 camping units, meeting rooms (478.3750, 478.3339).

EAST SHERMAN HOUSE, 311 E Sherman St., Hood River, 2-BR apt. wk. or month, wheelchair access, pets, Summer Season (386.3913).

HACKETT HOUSE, 922 State St. Hood River, bed & bfst. (386.1014).

HIDDEN COVES CAMPGROUND & RV PARK, Hwy 14, Stevenson WA 98648 (509.427.8098).

HOOD RIVER HOTEL, 102 Oak St. restored historic 41 unit hotel, wheelchair access (386.1900).

INN AT COOPER SPUR, 10755 Cooper Spur Rd., Mt.Hood-Parkdale, 23 mi. S Hood River, at 4000 ft. motel, dining (352.6692 — 800.344.4116).

INN AT THE GORGE, 1113 Eugene St., Hood River, bed & bfst apts., bus & Amtrak transport, windsurfing pkg., Summer Season (386.4429).

INN AT HOOD RIVER, 1108 Marina Way, 148-unit motel, dining, lounge, 7 days, on river (386.2200 — 800.828.7873).

LAKECLIFF ESTATE, 382 Westcliff Dr. Hood River, bed & bfst. (386.7000).

LONE PINE MOTEL, 2429 Cascade, Hood River 97031, 14 units (386.2601).

STATE STREET INN, 1005 State, Hood River, bed & bfst. (386.1899).

STEWART'S FARMHOUSE, 4077 Portland Dr. Hood Riv. bed & bfst (386.6343).

VAGABOND LODGE, 4070 Westcliff, Hood River, motel 25 units (386.2992).

Index